THE ORDER OF THE HOSPITAL OF ST. JOHN OF JERUSALEM

ST. JOHN'S GATE, FROM THE SOUTH, 1902.

THE ORDER
OF THE HOSPITAL OF
St. John of Jerusalem

BEING

A HISTORY OF THE ENGLISH HOSPITALLERS
OF ST. JOHN, THEIR RISE AND PROGRESS

BY

W. K. R. BEDFORD, M.A. Oxon.
GENEALOGIST OF THE ORDER

AND

RICHARD HOLBECHE, Lt.-Col.
LIBRARIAN OF THE ORDER

LONDON: F. E. ROBINSON AND CO.
20, GREAT RUSSELL STREET, BLOOMSBURY   1902

CHISWICK PRESS: CHARLES WHITTINGHAM AND CO.
TOOKS COURT, CHANCERY LANE, LONDON.

PREFACE

THE Editor desires to say a few, a very few, words of preface by way of explanation of the origin and object of the present volume.

Its inception commenced with a successful illustrated lecture delivered by Major Yate at the United Service Institution, which he wished the Order to reprint for general publication. The Council thought it expedient that the narrative should be somewhat enlarged, and circumstances preventing Major Yate from superintending the work, it was intrusted by the Council to the Genealogist, who again found it somewhat beyond his powers, and had to apply to the Librarian for assistance, especially in the later and more immediately interesting portions of the narrative, though retaining the general supervision of the whole.

The Editor would adopt as his own the apology of the author of the books of Maccabees: "If I have done well, and as is fitting the story, it is that which I desired; but if slenderly and meanly, it is that which I could attain unto."

Mr. H. W. Fincham has greatly assisted the work by his artistic photographs, as Mr. W. D. Scull has done by several drawings, and to Mr. Howe the book is indebted for the interesting figures from Siena.

Library of Congress Cataloging in Publication Data

Bedford, William Kirkpatrick Riland, 1826-1905.
   The Order of the Hospital of St. John of Jerusalem.

   Reprint of the 1902 ed. published by F. E. Robinson, London.
   Includes index.
   1. Grand Priory in the British Realm of the Most Venerable Order of the Hospital of St. John of Jerusalem. I. Holbeche, Richard, 1850-   joint author. II. Title.
CR4731.G7B4   1978   271'.79   79-29831
ISBN 0-404-15412-3

First AMS edition published in 1978.
Reprinted from the edition of 1902, London.

Trim Size:
   Original edition . 5-1/2 x 8-3/4
   AMS edition . . . 5-1/2 x 8-1/2

The text size of the original has been maintained in this edition.

MANUFACTURED IN THE UNITED STATES OF AMERICA

CONTENTS

	PAGE
CHAPTER I FOUNDATION OF THE ORDER	1
CHAPTER II CYPRUS AND RHODES	16
CHAPTER III THE ORDER IN ENGLAND	30
CHAPTER IV THE ORDER IN ENGLAND (*continued*)	55
CHAPTER V MALTA AND THE GREAT SIEGE	68
CHAPTER VI THE GRAND MASTERS OF MALTA	82
CHAPTER VII THE ENGLISH REVIVAL	98
CHAPTER VIII THE AMBULANCE MOVEMENT	112
CHAPTER IX THE CHARTER OF THE ENGLISH ORDER	139
CHAPTER X OPHTHALMIC HOSPITAL IN JERUSALEM	149

CONTENTS

CHAPTER XI
THE ST. JOHN AMBULANCE BRIGADE AND ITS SERVICES 165

APPENDIX A
RECEPTION OF A KNIGHT 181

APPENDIX B
COMMANDERIES OF THE ORDER OF ST. JOHN IN ENGLAND 183

APPENDIX C
GRAND PRIORS OF ENGLAND 185
TURCOPOLIERS OF THE ENGLISH LANGUAGE . 190
BAILLIS OF AQUILA, OR OF THE EAGLE . . 194
PRIORS OF IRELAND 198
PRIORS OF SCOTLAND 202

APPENDIX D
QUALIFICATION OF SIR ROBERT PEAT . . 205

APPENDIX E
DIGEST OF THE CHARTER 207

APPENDIX F
RECIPIENTS OF THE MEDALS OF THE ORDER . 209

INDEX 219

LIST OF ILLUSTRATIONS

	PAGE
ST. JOHN'S GATE, FROM THE SOUTH, 1902 *Frontispiece*	
GATEWAY TO MURISTAN . . . *Facing*	6
COSTUME OF THE ORDER. From frescoes at Siena . . . . . . *Facing*	8
STA. UBALDESCA . . . . . "	14
EARLY SEALS OF THE ORDER	15
CASTLE OF BUDRUM . . . . *Facing*	20
KNIGHTS MINISTERING TO THE SICK . "	22
EARTHQUAKE AT RHODES, 1480 . . "	22
THE HANGING OF MASTER GEORGE . "	24
THE MIRACULOUS VISION . . . "	24
ZYZYMY ENTERTAINED BY THE GRAND MASTER *Facing*	26
BAJAZET PRESENTS THE HAND OF ST. JOHN *Facing*	26
KILMAINHAM PRIORY: EAST FRONT . "	36
MONUMENT TO SIR WILLIAM WESTON "	48
HAND OF ST. JOHN IN ITS ORIGINAL CASE .	54
HOUSE OF THE HOSPITALLERS OF ST. JOHN OF JERUSALEM, CLERKENWELL . . *Facing*	56
THE CRYPT, NORTH TRANSEPT, AND THE NAVE OF THE CRYPT, ST. JOHN'S CHURCH, CLERKENWELL . . . . . . *Facing*	58
TORPHICHEN PRECEPTORY . . . "	66

LIST OF ILLUSTRATIONS

		PAGE
SIEGE OF MALTA. From old pictures	Facing	74
THE GREAT HOSPITAL AT MALTA	"	88
AUBERGE DE BAVIERE, MALTA	"	98
INSIGNIA OF KNIGHT OF JUSTICE AND KNIGHT OF GRACE	Facing	110
HAT AND SWORD OF LA VALLETTE		111
AMBULANCE WORKERS	Facing	120
THE CHALLENGE SHIELD	"	132
AUBERGE D'ANGLETERRE, MALTA		138
DUKE OF CLARENCE MEMORIAL TABLET		148
HOSPICE AT JERUSALEM	Facing	150
MEDAL AWARDED BY THE ORDER FOR SAVING LIFE ON LAND	Facing	210
TABLET IN ST. JOHN'S CHURCH, CLERKENWELL, TO DECEASED AMBULANCE VOLUNTEERS	Facing	216

HOSPITALLERS OF ST. JOHN

CHAPTER I

FOUNDATION OF THE ORDER

PRELIMINARY observations are generally uninteresting and undesirable : yet there are two points which suggest themselves as to the present work requiring a few words of comment. The first of these is, that it may be deemed almost unnecessary to produce another book upon a subject so thoroughly dealt with as the history of the Order of St. John has been by writers of high ability and reputation, especially in the comprehensive work of General Porter[1] and the able summary of the Rev. F. C. Woodhouse.[2] As the first mentioned of these valuable books, however, last saw the light in 1884, and the other appeared in 1879, the vast increase in the work and importance of the English Order since the spread of the Ambulance movement has excited a desire to know more about its rise and progress than

[1] "The Knights of Malta," by Major-General Whitworth Porter, 1884.
[2] "Military Religious Orders." S. P. C. K., 1879. Rev. F. C. Woodhouse.

either volume can satisfy; for the doings of the last ten years are the legitimate sequel of a chain of events dating back to the era of the first crusade, and the home of the Ambulance work in England is still that edifice which was originally founded for similar purposes in the twelfth century. This leads to the second observation, that little field for original authorship is left to be occupied. The statements of former writers have been repeatedly examined and tested; all that can be done at the present day is to repeat facts and to summarize narrative —to lead the reader to conclusions, by directing him to unimpeachable authorities.

With regard even to the dedication of the Order it would be possible to occupy space by referring to the controversies of the seventeenth century as to the legend of a hospital, called after the Asmonean prince John Hyrcanus, already existing in Jerusalem when the pious merchants of Amalfi began to establish their charitable design of a refuge for pilgrims, and hence the choice of St. John as patron; it, however, is now generally admitted that the St. John at first adopted as sponsor was the Greek patriarch John, distinguished by the epithet Eleemon, of whose career Mr. Duckworth has recently given a short sketch, and that it was to his charitable fame that the hospital owed its ascription.[1] This much, however, is certain, that by the time that the Crusading Army

[1] "St. John the Almsgiver," Rev. H. T. F. Duckworth, 1901.

FOUNDATION OF THE ORDER 3

under Godfrey of Bulloin captured the holy city from the Moslem, St. John the Baptist had been adopted as the patron saint of the Hospital;[1] and his image, already worn by patients suffering from epilepsy, became the authorized badge of those engaged in general hospital work.

The term hospital, however, did not for many years after this convey the idea of a building devoted to medical science alone, but more generally of a house of refuge. Thus the historian of Yorkshire says that at Hexton in that county was a "hospital" built in the time of King Athelstan for defending travellers from wolves, as is expressly stated in the public records.[2]

This hospice for the entertainment of wayfarers and the reception of the sick, which was in existence in 1099,[3] was naturally enough placed in as close vicinity as possible to those sacred spots to which tradition from the earliest ages of Christianity had caused the pious steps of pilgrims from every country

[1] Paciaudus, "De cultu S. Ioannis Baptistae." Rome, 1755.
[2] Southey's "Commonplace Book."
[3] The historian Ekkehard in 1101 asserts that Jerusalem was never since the days of John Hyrcanus without a hospital, and there is evidence that the French Benedictines worked in a hospice founded by St. Gregory in 603; while Charlemagne nearly two centuries later claimed the title of protector of the pilgrims to Jerusalem, but it is acknowledged that the building of the citizens of Amalfi was erected on the ruins of this foundation.— "De prima origine Hospitaliorum," J. Delaville La Roulx. Paris, 1885.

of the West to be directed. For thirty-four years before this, from the period of the capture of Jerusalem by the Turcomans, pilgrimage had assumed a new phase in Palestine. In addition to the incommodities inseparable from distant travel in semi-barbarous regions, pilgrims were ill-treated by the new masters of the soil. The very permission to enter the city and view the Holy Sepulchre depended on the caprice or the covetousness of a Turkish chief, so that many unfortunate persons who had sold everything to enable them to make the pilgrimage to Zion, after enduring the hardship of the long voyage, the sickness, robbery, and other dangers of the way, found themselves at the gates of Jerusalem without sufficient money to gain an entrance, and were obliged to return without a sight of the object of their arduous undertaking; or possibly died of want, uncared for and friendless, without reward for their labour and suffering. Save for the assistance afforded by Gerard, the first administrator of the Hospital, and his associates, pilgrimage would have been an impossibility, owing to the hardships and indignities to which the devout Christians were exposed.

The original buildings of the Hospital were probably meagre, but ere long they enlarged their bounds to the extent thus described by Porter:

"To the south of the church of the Holy Sepulchre there is a plot of ground nearly square, about

FOUNDATION OF THE ORDER 5

five hundred feet a side, which is bounded on the north by what was formerly the Street of Palmers, now known as the Via Dolorosa; on the west by Patriarch Street, now Christian Street; on the south by Temple Street, now David Street; and on the east by the Malquinat or Bazaar. Within this area stood the later buildings of the Order. North of the Street of Palmers and to the east of the Church of the Holy Sepulchre, stood the churches and hospitals of St. Mary ad Latinos and St. Mary Magdalene (also ad Latinos), the original establishments of the Amalfi merchants. To the south of the Street of Palmers, in the western angle of the square, stood the church of St. John Eleemon and its hospice."[1]

Such was the situation as it existed prior to the formation of the kingdom of Jerusalem in 1099. Between that time and the middle of the twelfth century the Order under Raymond du Puy had developed the church of St. John Eleemon into a fine building, the conventual church of St. John the Baptist. On the east of that they had erected another large church called Santa Maria Majora with a monastic quadrangle to the south of it, and along the south of the whole square looking towards Temple Street ran the noble hospital of St. John. When Jerusalem was captured by Saladin, the church of St. John the Baptist was by the Saracens converted into a madhouse (in Turkish Muristan). "The

[1] See "Transactions of Palestine Exploration Society," 1902.

6 HOSPITALLERS OF ST. JOHN

Muristan" was granted to Germany in 1869, but a view of the gateway of St. John as it appeared before that year is taken from Pierotti's "Jerusalem." Together with a local habitation the Hospitallers gained from the Christian kingdom of Jerusalem a constitution. Gerard was appointed first Master, having been one of the prominent members of the old charitable guild, if not the originator of the Hospice, though the latter supposition is scarcely credible if we adopt the date usually assigned by historians of 1048. Raymond du Puy succeeded to the Mastership in 1118, at which time Baldwin II. was the Latin King of Jerusalem. The Hospital had been recognized by the Archbishop of Caesarea in 1112, and had much increased in credit and useful work. Baldwin, however, was anxious to stamp upon it a military character (as was also done upon the Order of the Temple in 1130), and it seems probable that the circumstances of the time, the Latin kingdom of Jerusalem, a small and isolated territory, being day by day more continuously beset by its Mahometan enemies, rendered it a matter of necessity that its adherents of every grade should take up arms in its defence. Under its new organization the Order was divided into three classes, first of whom in rank and position were the Knights of Justice. Admission to this grade was only given to those who could produce satisfactory proofs of the nobility of their descent. Every candidate must have already received the

GATEWAY TO MURISTAN.
From Pierotti's "Jerusalem."

FOUNDATION OF THE ORDER

accolade of knighthood from secular hands, before he could be enrolled as a Knight of Justice in the Order of St. John. The second class comprised the strictly ecclesiastical portion of the convent, and was eventually subdivided into two distinct grades, the Conventual Chaplains, who performed the religious functions of the Order at Headquarters, and the Priests of Obedience, who carried on similar duties in other priories and commanderies of the Order throughout Europe. The third class were denominated Serving Brothers; these too were subdivided into two grades—the Servants at arms or Esquires, and the Servants at office. The Servants at arms performed the duties of Esquires under the Knights of Justice, and if they were eligible became in due time enrolled among their number. The Servants at office were men of a lower class in life, who performed the duties of domestics within the convent and hospital. This class, though wanting the position and dignity of their nobler brethren, possessed numerous privileges and emoluments which rendered admission into the Order even in this grade very advantageous to men of the humbler ranks of society.

The habit was a black robe with a cowl, having a cross of eight points in white linen upon the left breast. This at first was worn by all Hospitallers to whichever of the three classes they belonged, but at a later period (under Pope Alexander IV.) the combatant knights were distinguished by a white cross upon a ground gules. The first appearance of a force of Hospitaller knights in active warfare was certainly at Antioch in 1119, and the details of the military constitution of the Order of St. John were complete in 1128. The two colleges of military knights, known respectively as the Temple and the Hospital, remained, during the rest of the history of the Christian monarchy in the Holy Land, the chief prop of its tottering throne: much jealousy, however, existed between the rival Orders, and the Hospital had not only to defend itself from its avowed enemies without, but from the intrigues and conspiracies within the Christian ranks, aggravated by the jealousy of the regular clergy, who were offended by the patronage extended by the Sovereign Pontiff to these military clerics, as well as to the similar corps of the Teutonic knights and knights of St. Lazarus. That in all these quarrels and jealousies the Order of the Hospital was invariably in the right would be absurd to assert, but it may be said, and supported even by the testimony of their opponents, that its members never lost sight of the charitable and hospitable purposes for which they had been originally incorporated, and that they were never disgraced by that treacherous correspondence with the enemy of which at times members of other professing Christian bodies were confessedly guilty. The ever increasing disunion among the

IN ARMOUR. ALBERTO ARRINGHIERI, KNIGHT OF ST. JOHN. IN BLACK MANTLE.

From frescoes by Pinturicchio in Siena Cathedral.

FOUNDATION OF THE ORDER

Christian communities led, however, to the capitulation of Jerusalem in 1187, and deprived the Order of St. John of that home which for upwards of a century had been a shelter not only to their own people but to all whose needs demanded aid. The buildings, which had risen in extent and beauty since the first foundation by the Amalfi brethren, once more reverted to the Moslem, in whose hands they remained until they fell into ruin.

The members of the Order betook themselves straightway to a town and castle called Margat; and when the third crusade, in which our English King Richard Cœur de Lion bore so prominent a part, had captured the ancient city of Ptolemais, they established their headquarters there, from which the town derived its later name of St. Jean d'Acre; this was in 1192, and it continued to be their abode for close upon a century. Admitting that worldly policy and rivalry with other conventual bodies had somewhat besmirched their ancient fame, the Hospitallers were still held in such general estimation that, after the capture of Jerusalem, Sultan Saladin not only granted them possession of their convent and hospital for another year in order that the charitable work might not be too rudely interrupted, but even made, as is reported, liberal donations towards that work. One who was not likely to be desirous of unduly praising a rival Order, Thierry, Grand Master of the Templars, gave in a letter to Henry II. of England the following report of the events of that period:

"Know, great king, that Saladin has taken the city of Jerusalem and the tower of David: the Syrian Christians are allowed to guard the Holy Sepulchre only till the fourth day after next Michaelmas: and the Hospitallers are permitted to stay a year longer in their house to take care of the sick. The knights of that Order who are in the castle of Beauvoir distinguish themselves every day by their various enterprises against the Saracens. They have lately taken two caravans from the infidels, in the first of which they found the arms and ammunition which the Turks were transporting from the fortress of La Fere after they had demolished it. Carac, in the neighbourhood of Mount Royal, Mount Royal itself, Sapheta of the Temple, another Carac, and Margat which belongs to the Hospitallers, Castel Blanco, Tripoli, and Antioch still hold out against the efforts of the Turks. Saladin has caused the great cross to be taken down from the dome of the church that was built on the ground of Solomon's temple, and for two days together it was dragged ignominiously through the streets, trampled under foot, and defiled with dirt. They have washed the inside and outside of that church with rose-water by way of purification, in order to make a mosque of it, and there they have solemnly proclaimed the law of Mahomet. The Turks have laid siege to Tyre ever since

FOUNDATION OF THE ORDER

Martinmas, a great number of military engines play upon it night and day, throwing in continually square stones of vast bigness. Young Conrad, son of the Marquis of Monserrat, has shut himself up in the place and makes a gallant defence, being well seconded by the knights of St. John and the Templars. On the eve of St. Silvester[1] seventeen Christian galleys with these brave friars on board sailed out of port, with ten Sicilian vessels commanded by General Margarit, a Catalan by nation, and attacked the fleet of Saladin in a manner before his eyes. The infidels were defeated. The great admiral of Alexandria and eight Emirs were made prisoners. They took eleven ships and a great number ran aground on the coast, which Saladin set on fire and burnt to ashes, for fear they should fall into the hands of the Christians. That prince appeared the next day in his camp, mounted on the finest of his horses, whose tail and ears he had cut off, making thus a public acknowledgment of the defeat he had received and of the trouble it gave him."[2]

I have quoted this passage at length because it contains a tribute to the Order from an impartial source, not only as to the value of their hospital work, but also as to their having already become proficient in that naval warfare which was ultimately to raise them to the position of maintainers of the

[1] December 30th.   [2] Woodhouse, p. 36.

peace of the Mediterranean Sea, a position to which the English navy has succeeded.

It is to be feared that the luxury and licence which characterized the Christian occupation of Acre had a deleterious influence upon the discipline of the Order. The Templars and Hospitallers turned their swords against one another, the Order of the Temple being jealous of the superior wealth of their rivals. Matthew Paris, the historian, estimates at this period the property of the Hospital at 19,000 manors and of the Temple at only 9,000. The soil of Palestine was dyed with fraternal blood at Margat and elsewhere, and the result was encouragement to the mutual enemy of both Orders.

Nor was the morality of Acre in the days of its prosperity at all what a Christian capital ought to have exhibited. Each race and division of the Latins, people of seventeen different countries speaking different languages and governed by different laws, occupied a separate and distinct portion of the town, having no community of interest with each other and rendering allegiance to no common supreme head. Every species of vice and extravagance consequently flourished unchecked, and the general demoralization was such that the city became a perfect sink of iniquity.

The Pope, who had but a short time before come forward as the defender of the Knights Hospitallers from the high-handed censure of the Emperor

FOUNDATION OF THE ORDER 13

Frederick and borne testimony to their good service, took occasion, in addressing the Grand Master de Comps in 1238, to accuse the knights generally, on authority which he asserts to be undeniable, of harbouring within their convents women of loose character, of possessing individually private property, despite their vow of poverty, of assisting the enemies of the Church with horses and arms, and of other crimes. Yet on the other hand we have the testimony of many eminent soldiers and ecclesiastics to the merit and charitable piety of individual members of the Order, and a general concurrence in the view that if it needed reformation it was still maintaining, comparatively speaking, the promise of its earlier day. Pope Alexander (1259) confessed that the Order suffered a disadvantage from the want of a distinctive garb, which made it easy for those who were not professed to pass themselves off as knights of the Hospital, and for those who had joined the Order and lost their first love for its work to evade their obligations. He therefore granted to the Master and brethren permission to decree and make inviolate the regulation, that the knights should wear black mantles "that they may be distinguished from the other brethren" and in campaigns, and in battle should wear surcoats of a red colour, with a cross of white, in accordance with that on the standard. This command relates, it must be observed, to the Knights of Justice only. The Convent then consisted but of three classes—knights, clerics, and servitors. Ladies now were added, and took their share in the charitable employment of the Hospital and rivalled in religious zeal the most sanctified of the brethren. Three hundred years after this, in the Grand Mastership of Cardinal Verdala, the remains of one of these holy women, St. Ubaldesca, were transported to Malta, and received all the honours due to the relics of a Saint.

The King of Hungary thus describes his impression after visiting some of the principal houses of the knights : " Lodging in their house I have seen them feed every day an innumerable multitude of poor, the sick laid in good beds and treated with great care, the dying assisted with an exemplary piety, and the dead buried with proper decency. In a word, the Knights of St. John are employed, sometimes like Mary in contemplation and sometimes like Martha in action, and this noble militia consecrate their days either in their infirmaries or else in engagements against the enemies of the cross."

Whatever deterioration may have affected the morals and discipline of the Hospitallers at Acre, it is sufficiently clear from history that it had not, like Capua with Hannibal's soldiers, enervated their courage. The gathering storm of Saracen success burst upon the devoted city at last : the rivalry between Templar and Hospitaller was merged in the effort on the part of each to outshine the other

STA. UBALDESCA.

From the portrait at St. John's Gate, presented to the Order by Sir Victor Houlton.

FOUNDATION OF THE ORDER

in daring and endurance. Again and again were the hordes of Orientals repulsed by the diminishing but undaunted band of soldier monks; and, though it is almost impossible to say who of the devoted garrison had the honour to prolong the resistance to the last, yet John de Villiers, Grand Master, and his few surviving knights, we are assured, left no combatants behind them when they had fought their way to their boats and hoisted sail in their galleys for a port of refuge in the island of Cyprus.

EARLY SEALS OF THE ORDER

CHAPTER II

CYPRUS AND RHODES

THE island of Cyprus was not on the whole a suitable place for the headquarters of the Order. Limasol was no fort of strength; and the claims of the king of the island prevented the knights from having as free a hand as they desired. They determined to find a better place of rendezvous; and, though at first baffled in their attempts, in 1310, under Fulco de Villaret, 24th Grand Master, they accomplished the capture of the island of Rhodes, in climate and situation exactly what they required. Its fertile soil, fine harbour, and vicinity to the mainland were strong recommendations, and the growing importance of the Order rendered the nominal suzerainty of the Greek emperor a mere shade, which passed away even before the fall of the Empire itself. Forts and hospitals soon arose side by side, and Christian refugees were brought from provinces subdued by Turkish arms to aid in forming a bulwark against Mahometan conquest. A fleet of galleys, which had been commenced at Cyprus, assumed formidable dimensions in the new harbour, and effectually checked the supremacy of the Turkish corsairs.

CYPRUS AND RHODES

Much of the ability to carry out these designs for the general weal of Christendom was derived from the aggrandizement of the Order of St. John at the expense of their old rivals, allies, and enemies, the Templars. When the two fraternities quitted the soil of the Holy Land the knights of the Temple, holding that all prospect of the fulfilment of their original vow to protect the Holy places was at an end, at once betook themselves to their European preceptories, and became obnoxious to the governments under which they settled by the wealth and oriental ostentation which, like the Nabobs of a later day, they brought into social and political life. Their enemies only waited until public feeling had been sufficiently excited to render their destruction an easy task. The Pope and the King of France (Clement V. and Philip the Fair) took the lead in a campaign of extermination carried out with ruthless barbarity. The kings and nobility of the various countries in which the Templars flourished fell upon the rich spoil thus thrown into their hands, but the Pope interposed to restrain the total secularization of such enormous revenues, and therefore a considerable portion of the property of the Templars was ultimately conferred upon the Order of St. John, who were considered to have earned it by their praiseworthy determination to maintain inviolate those obligations which could only be fulfilled by continued stay in some Eastern city such as Rhodes, where they remained an abiding menace to the infidel and a moral support to Christendom. It was at this time (the beginning of the fourteenth century) that the Order was divided into *Langues*. Hitherto the native of each country had been received into a cosmopolitan Brotherhood embracing all Christendom. Now, without disturbing in any degree the distinctive organization of the three classes of Knights, Chaplains, and Serving Brothers, a new classification was created, upon the principle of nationality, to supplement the former. The Order was divided into the seven nations or tongues of Provence, Auvergne, France, Italy, Aragon, England, and Germany. To these seven an eighth was subsequently added to increase the Spanish influence in their councils. The Langue of Aragon was divided, the new moiety taking the title of the Langue of Castile and embracing Portugal. At the same time the chief dignities of the Order were severally appropriated to the principals of the various nations, who from being bound to reside at the headquarters of the Order became a kind of Privy Council for the Grand Master, and were termed Conventual Bailiffs. The Conventual Bailiff of Provence was thus *ex officio* styled the Grand Commander; that of Auvergne the Marshal; of France the Grand Hospitaller; of Italy the Admiral; of Aragon the Grand Conservator; of England the Turcopolier, or Commander of the cavalry; of Germany the High Bailiff,

CYPRUS AND RHODES

and of Castile the High Chancellor. Various forts in the new line of defences of the city of Rhodes were placed under the charge of one of these divisions, and presently each Langue erected for itself an Auberge (lodging quarters) with mess-room, etc., for its own members. It must, however, be understood that no member nor even officer was absolutely and of necessity a subject of the government of the country designated by the title of the Langue. Thus Scotland, for instance, while an independent kingdom, was a contributory to the treasury of the Turcopolier, the Prior of Clerkenwell, while some Scotsmen were members of one or other of the Langues which took their designation from France.

Speaking of Rhodes as a residence in every way desirable, we do not forget the legend which ascribes to the young adventurous knight De Gozon, afterwards Grand Master of the Order, the destruction of a dragon which ravaged the interior of the island. Prosaic historians would interpret such feats into the draining of marshes and cure of malarial disease. Remembering, however, that the Greek name of the island signified the Isle of Serpents, and that the skull and backbone of some enormous animal, apparently of the ophidian species, hung over one of the gates of the city until they were destroyed by an earthquake in 1830, we may admit at least the outline of the story dramatized by Schiller and rendered by the pencil of Retzsch. And while we may demur to the portraiture of "English bulldogs," the fidelity of the pictures is generally apparent.

It would seem that the two posts of the greatest practical importance were held by the French and Italian Conventual Bailiffs. The very salt which kept sweet the reputation of the Order was that it ever esteemed the redemption of the captive and the succour of the sick its primary objects. Before its ships afforded protection to the commerce of the Mediterranean, hundreds of Christian slaves laboured to death in giving wings to the fleets of their oppressors; but when the Rhodian galleys turned the tables, the daring pirate from Algiers or Goleta often found himself condemned to take the place of his quondam captive. For these rescued folk, "wasted with misery," the knights provided every comfort, and the best medical skill then attainable. An engraving from William de Cavorsin's account of the Order in the fifteenth century represents the scene which was part of the everyday life of the Convent. Rhodes itself was peopled in a great degree by Christian refugees, bound by the ties of gratitude and interest to the Order. Its vicinity to the mainland, and the capture of Smyrna in the middle of the fourteenth century, rendered such objects comparatively easy of accomplishment; and even after Smyrna had fallen into the hands of Timour the Tartar, with the loss of its entire garrison, the Order erected, partly with

CASTLE OF BUDRUM.

CYPRUS AND RHODES

materials derived from the Mausoleum of Halicarnassus, a stately castle, which still stands, a specimen of their skill in military architecture, called to this day Budrum, from Bedros (Peter), a Rock. In this fortalice, which Grand Master de Naillac erected at the end of a peninsula jutting out into the Mediterranean, in the juncture when the power of the rival Moslem leaders Bajazet and Timour had for the time ceased to be threatening, any unfortunate Christian flying from slavery was certain to find ample and hospitable protection. As aids to its defence a race of fine dogs was kept within the castle, whose natural instinct became so developed by training, that they not only gave early intimation of the approach of enemies, but performed, towards Christian refugees, the same devices of intelligent rescue which the dogs of St. Bernard at a later period were credited with in the care of Alpine travellers.

Scattered about the castle are the armorial bearings of its successive captains from 1437 to 1522, when the garrison surrendered to the Turks. Among these is the name of a well-known English knight, Sir Thomas Sheffield, with the date 1514. The arms of another Englishman, John Kendal, who was Turcopolier 1477-1500, may be seen under the Royal arms (of Edward IV.) on the tower at the south-east angle. Here, as at Rhodes, the stern monotony of military masonry is constantly relieved by shields and inscriptions sculptured in white marble and let into the walls. There are indeed several mementos of English knights in the later period of the occupation of Rhodes by the Order. No doubt many members of the English Langue were of foreign extraction, and no doubt also the strange phonetic spelling of some of our English proper names prevents us from recognizing them in the histories; but the presumption is also strong that English soldiers preferred to take their share of the fighting which was going on at home, to the distant and less immediately interesting war in the Mediterranean. Those who joined the headquarters of the Order would be useful and prominent enough—the stuff of which our adventurers have always been made—but they would soon be aweary of the routine which would ensue when active operations were not going on, and had, as we discover from various sources, a knack of becoming discontented and impatient. Towards the end of the fifteenth century, however, at a time when the war with France had ceased, and the house of York seemed firmly settled on the throne, a state of things arose at Rhodes which required all the energy and fighting power which the Grand Master could summon from the most distant communities of his confraternity. The progress made by the naval power of the Order had, for considerably over a century, excited the alarm and hostility of the Sultan of Turkey. In the earlier stages of the settlement at Rhodes some desultory attacks on the island had

KNIGHTS MINISTERING TO THE SICK.
From Cavorsin.

EARTHQUAKE AT RHODES, 1480.
From Cavorsin.

CYPRUS AND RHODES

been undertaken with no success. Now, however, after the Grand Turk, Mahomet II., in 1453 had taken the city of Constantinople, the garrison of Rhodes knew that an attack upon them would only be a question of time, and commenced energetic movements to meet the coming danger. During the successive reigns of Grand Masters de Milly, Zacosta, and Orsini, constant assaults were made upon the outlying fortalices of the Order, though in most cases unsuccessfully; and in 1470, when the island of Negropont was subdued by Mahomet, a general summons to Rhodes was issued to all the members of the Order in the remoter countries. A treaty between the Christian powers and Persia, which led to a war with the Sultan, interposed for a time; but in 1476, when it was evident that the crisis was at hand, Peter d'Aubusson, a tried soldier of great experience, who had just fortunately succeeded to the baton of Grand Master, began to take prompt and vigorous steps for the defence of the city and island. The storm burst in May, 1480, when a force of at least 80,000 men in 160 ships succeeded in effecting a landing on the coast. It would appear that the enterprise was much encouraged by renegade traitors, the Turkish general himself being a member of the Greek family of Paleologos who had embraced Ismalism. But the most astute and daring of these rascals was one George Frapant, a German engineer, whose scheme was to pretend a desertion from the

Turkish army, and thus to gain admission within the walls of the city, where he could act as a spy and communicate with his allies outside. Fortunately the Grand Master placed no reliance upon him from the first, and strict surveillance brought his designs to light, so that he was hanged before the termination of the siege, which lasted till the 27th of July.

The principal object of attack was the huge tower of St. Michael, which guarded the port, and after a tremendous cannonade a boat assault was made and repulsed with heavy loss. The enemy then turned their attention to the Ghetto, in a part of the town where the ramparts were weak, and succeeded in mining some of the defences. Countermines, however, defeated this effort, and another great attack on St. Michael was foiled by an English sailor, Roger Jervis, who cut adrift a floating bridge which had been constructed to carry the column of assailants. The loss of the Turks in this abortive attempt was enormous: so when a plot to assassinate the Grand Master had also failed, and the Basha heard that Master George had met with his deserts, only the chance of an escalade of the wall near the Jews' quarter remained.

So terrific a bombardment was brought to bear at this point, that the defenders were for a short time driven from the wall, and the Turkish host, swarming up a facile breach, took possession of the defences, leaving the Rhodian garrison to retake them

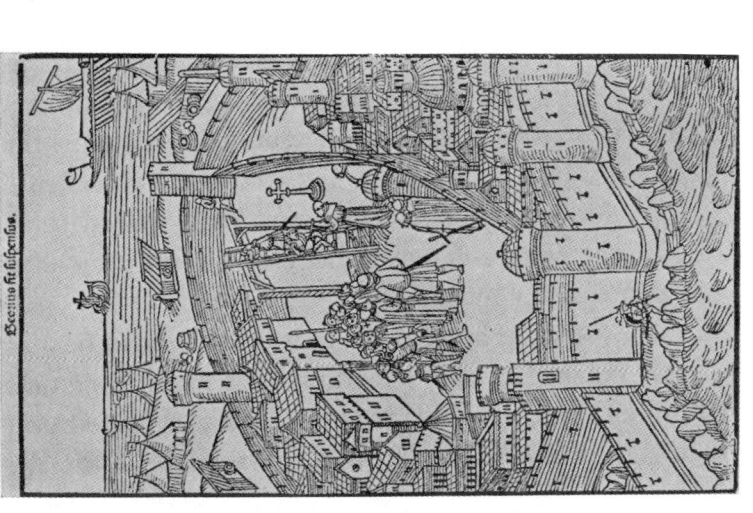

THE HANGING OF MASTER GEORGE.
From Cavorsin.

THE MIRACULOUS VISION.
From Cavorsin.

from within. This, however, they contrived to do, most gallantly led by the Grand Master and his brother, who had brought a force to his aid. Three thousand five hundred Turks fell in this decisive combat, of which we have a vivid description from the pen of William de Cavorsin, Chancellor of the Order, in a chronicle, 1496, translated into English by John Kaye, Laureate to King Edward IV., and published by Caxton under the title of "The delectable News and Tidings of the glorious victory of the Rhodians against the Turks."

The pious chronicler William de Cavorsin seems to have entertained no doubt of the miraculous character of this repulse. These are his words: "By the commandment of the Lord Master a banner of Jesu Christ, another of Our Lady, and another of St. John Baptist, patron of the Order of Rhodes, were set upon the walls when the battle was on both sides most sharp. And anon after the Turks saw properly in the midst of the clear and bright air a cross all shining gold, and also saw a bright virgin which had in her hands against the host of the Turks a spear and a shield, and on that sight also appeared a man clothed in poor and vile array, which was accompanied with great number of fair and well-beseen men in arms, as if he would have come down to the help of Rhodes. By the cross of gold we may justly understand our Saviour Jesu Christe: and by the Virgin we may understand

Our Lady the Blessed Mary: and by the man poorly clothed we may understand the Holy Saint John Baptist, Patron and Avowere of the Order of Rhodes, which was accompanied with saints and angels of God for to help the Rhodians. The which godly and heavenly sight put plainly the Turks in so great wonder and fear."[1]

In the same year, 1480, Rhodes suffered severely from an earthquake, and Mahomet cherished a design of renewing the struggle, which was frustrated by his death, when his sons Bajazet and Zizim disputed the succession. Bajazet obtained the mastery, whereupon Zizim, after several romantic adventures, threw himself upon the hospitality of the Knights, who, considering him a dangerous guest, yet unwilling to give him up to his brother, sent him to France, to the custody of Charles VIII. The French King handed him over to Pope Alexander VI. (Borgia) in 1488. He did not survive the transfer long.[2] It was at this period that Bajazet made a truce with the Order, and presented

---

[1] "The Dylectable Newesse and Tithynges of the gloryous victorye of the Rhodyans agaynst the Turkes." Caxton, Westminster, 1490.

[2] "This Pope, among the many evil deeds of his infamous life, set himself to interfere with the independence of the Order of St. John. Claiming to have a right to dispose of all the dignities of the Order, he appointed a nephew to a commandery in Aragon, although the Grand Master had already nominated an illustrious knight of that province."—WOODHOUSE.

BAJAZET PRESENTS THE HAND OF ST. JOHN.

From Cavorsin.

ZYZYMY ENTERTAINED BY THE GRAND MASTER.

From Cavorsin.

CYPRUS AND RHODES

them with the great relic, the hand of St. John, which had been captured by the Turks at Constantinople.

D'Aubusson died in 1503. His successor, D'Amboise, built the fine gateway still to be seen at Rhodes, and died in 1512.

On the death of Grand Master Carretto in 1521, a keen contest ensued between two distinguished knights, D'Amiral and L'Isle Adam, which was determined in favour of the latter, to the intense chagrin of D'Amiral.

Solyman the Magnificent, who had succeeded Selim as Sultan in 1522, now determined upon another effort to capture Rhodes, and on the 26th June of that year landed 100,000 soldiers and 60,000 pioneers. Two large earthworks were constructed to command the towers of St. Mary and of Italy (the latter the Jews' quarter), and a series of assaults took place of a similar character to those in the former siege. The great attacks were made on the 13th and 24th of September, but with a garrison of 4,000 only, L'Isle Adam repulsed both. The Sultan was much disheartened, and publicly disgraced his generals.

Within the city itself famine and disaffection were increasing. The native population clamoured for surrender, and sought terms for themselves. D'Amiral was brought to trial for treasonable correspondence with the enemy, found guilty, and executed, though his complicity seems at least "not proven." L'Isle Adam repulsed another assault on December 17th, but in spite of this temporary success he had to sign a capitulation on honourable terms, and the Knights left the island on January 1st, 1523, and once more were homeless. The Mussulman history of this siege is extant, and agrees in all essential particulars with the records of the Order.

The terms on which Rhodes was surrendered were more favourable than the Sultan had ever granted in a capitulation before, and they were doubtless granted out of the admiration which he felt for the character of Grand Master L'Isle Adam, to whom he proffered the highest honours and dignities if he would enter the service of the Crescent, and when informed in return that such a change of principles was impossible, the Sultan could not forbear the expression of his warm admiration for so great a man. "I cannot help being concerned," he added, "that I force this Christian at his age to go out of his house," and went on to speak with bitter contempt of the Christian kings who had left this noble soldier without aid in his extremity. Nearly 5,000 knights and Rhodians left the island with the Grand Master, the Order having ruled there for 220 years.

For seven years they were homeless, having first taken up their quarters at their Priory of Messina,

CYPRUS AND RHODES

where the Grand Master's immediate care was to provide for those who were sick and wounded. He waited on them himself, assisted by the knights who were left unhurt. Soon after this they were driven from Messina by an outbreak of plague, and by the permission of Pope Clement VII. (de Medici), who had been Bishop of Worcester, and was a member of the Order of St. John, they took up quarters for a while in the city of Viterbo while the Grand Master began to search for a new home, Malta, which had been offered by the Emperor Charles V., not being favoured. Among other courts he visited that of England, where at his instance King Henry VIII. abandoned for the time an intention which he had expressed of confiscating the property of the Order. More than one abortive attempt was made to acquire the city of Modon in Greece; but when the last of these in 1530 had failed, L'Isle Adam recognized the necessity of fitting Malta to the requirements of the Order, and died in harness in the castle of St. Angelo, where a tablet still marks his original burying-place, though his bones were afterwards removed to St. John's by G. M. de la Cassiere.

CHAPTER III

THE ORDER IN ENGLAND

ALMOST contemporaneously with the complete establishment of the Order in Palestine, a branch was formed in England, where Jordain Briset founded a house for the purposes of the Hospital in Clerkenwell early in the twelfth century. Before the century closed a church had been consecrated by Heraclius, Patriarch of Jerusalem (1185), and a Priory established. In 1180 the Ladies of the Order were housed at Buckland in Somersetshire, and were joined there after the capture of Jerusalem by those who had hitherto been attached to the hospital at headquarters.

The sisters of Buckland (says Mr. Hugo), though constantly numbering in their community the daughters of great and noble houses, were but slenderly supported, and for a long time at least far from adequately provided for. They were considered also in the light of a burden and grievance by the officers charged in a special degree with their direction and general well-being. At first consisting but of a Prioress and nine sisters, the Society

THE ORDER IN ENGLAND

amounted in the year 1338 to fifty ladies, who together with their servants must have needed a considerable revenue. Doubtless a great part of the cost of their maintenance was defrayed by contributions from the charitable of the neighbourhood and more distant friends. Their precise relationship to the Order of St. John has been, Mr. Hugo thinks, greatly misunderstood.[1] Tanner says that "they had at first great dependence on the knights, but afterward they discharged themselves and became a distinct Priory or Hospital of Nuns of the Order of St. Augustine, and there is no mention of their being subordinate to any other Religions."[2] On the contrary, their Chaplain and Steward were always officers of the Order, and they received their ancient pensions and were accounted *obedientiariae* down to the period of the dissolution. That the Priory was distinct from the Commandery as a religious community is of course certain, for it was the very reason of its foundation that the Sisterhood should be thus separated. But their union with the Order itself was never apparently broken. The fact that they were called Nuns of the Order of St. Augustine is not to be understood as militating against this view, inasmuch as the Hospitallers, as well as the Templars, were members of that numerous body of

---

[1] Hugo, "History of Mynchin Buckland."
[2] "Notitia Monastica."

conventual societies which accepted the rule of St. Austin as the guide of their religious life.[1]

The names of the first sisters lodged at what was hereafter called Nuns Buckland have been preserved. They were nine in number—Sister Millisent, previously living at Sterndon, Herts; Sister Johanna, at Hamton, Middlesex; Sister Basilia, at Kerebrooke, Norfolk; Sister Amabilia and Sister Amicia, at Malketon, at Thenegay, Cambridge; Sister Christina, at Hoggeshawe, Bucks; Sister Petronilla, at Gosford, Oxon; and Sister Agnes, at Clanefelde, in the same county. They were located at Buckland that, as it was solemnly added, they and their successors might serve God in that place for ever. Such was the small beginning of this afterwards famous Sisterhood.[2]

We learn from one of the Cottonian MSS. that the first Prioress was named Fina. This lady, who died about the year 1240, governed the house for the long space of sixty years, and outlived from the date of her appointment seven successive heads of the Order. She was greatly revered and remembered in the prayers of the Sisterhood long after her decease.[3] Gilbert de Vere, Prior of Clerkenwell, gave the sisters an annual pension of 100 shillings.

At Malta scarcely anything relating to the English members of the Order is preserved. One very

---

[1] Hugo, "Mynchin Buckland," pp. 51-52.
[2] Ditto, MS. in Coll. Arm. C. 17, f. 153.
[3] Ditto, MS. Cott. Nero, E. vi. f. 457b.

THE ORDER IN ENGLAND 33

remarkable exception, however, is to be made. The Rev. L. B. Larking, a Kentish antiquary, during a visit to Malta, discovered a copy of an "extent," or valuation of the property of the Order in England in 1338, as reported to the Grand Master, Elyan de Villanova, by Priors Thomas L'Archer and Leonard de Tybertis. Mr. Larking had this important document copied, and finally it was printed by the Camden Society with an admirable and erudite preface by Mr. Kemble, from which we may take the liberty of quoting at some length. He starts by calling attention to the principle of all the half-clerical, half-military Orders, which was to have a concentration of government of their own, an *imperium in imperio* everywhere. " The practice was to establish brotherhoods everywhere dependent upon other brotherhoods, but the idea to be ultimately realized was unity, not nationality. In some of the associations this unity rested in the Pope, but more generally in the Masters of the Orders, whom the Pope detested, because under favourable circumstances the Master might himself possibly become a Pope. The Universal Church did not like improvements upon its system, beginning with asceticism and ending in rival kingship, any more than the clergyman of this or that neighbourhood looks favourably upon a total abstinence movement which professes to make men wiser and better than Christianity itself can make them. The Pope in truth liked Templars and

Hospitallers no better than the vicar likes the Ranter or Baptist, and had much the same feeling towards the preceptory as a good churchman towards Ebenezer."

Yet, as Mr. Kemble confesses, we might be nearly sure, even if we had not the positive evidence of history, that the arrangements of the Order were adapted in every land to the exigencies and accidents of their position. In Syria they encamped; in Rhodes they fortified; in France and England they simply farmed and amassed money for the general purposes of the ruling body. So England, the country most remote from headquarters, was apt to think less of the personal duties of military service to the central authority than of the payment of the allotted share of the expenses; and the English participants in the defence of Rhodes might be easily reckoned, while the Prior of Kilmainham, sixty years before, had gone at the head of 1,500 Irish infantry to the invasion of France.

The volume, from the preface to which we just now quoted, contains a complete catalogue of all the property possessed by the Order of St. John in England in the year 1338—"a balance sheet for every manor, containing a strict account of profit and loss, and so arranged as to show at a glance what sum was available after all charges were deducted for the general purposes of the priory and the Order." A record, in fact, of income and expenditure. On

THE ORDER IN ENGLAND 35

the first head, in every commandery we find, to begin with, a mansion with its kitchen garden and orchard, negative rather than positive sources of income, yet with something to be carried to the credit side; the dovecote also furnishing a small item of gain : next comes the rent received for arable and meadow land, of which the former varied from two shillings an acre in Lincoln and Kent, down to three halfpence in Somerset and Norfolk; while meadow land varied from two to three shillings only. For pasture, the head of cattle fed upon it fixed the value; the keep of a cow being two shillings, an ox or a horse one shilling, a calf sixpence, a sheep a penny, a goat three farthings.

The unappropriated rectorial tithes of parish churches served by vicars or chaplains were also a source of profit to the Treasury of the Order : compulsory service of tenants (commuted generally for a money payment of twopence a day) brought in considerable revenue.

There also existed an item called *confraria*, a voluntary contribution collected from the pious neighbours. The sum thus collected in 1338 amounted to £888 4s. 3d. for all England.

The Order had establishments in twenty-six English counties and in Wales—a list of these will be found in an appendix. Several of them (with an income of £1,000 per annum in the aggregate) had been preceptories of the Templars, handed over to the

Hospitallers when the Order of the Temple had been dissolved. In Scotland the Order had been planted by King David I., who in 1124 established a preceptory at Torphichen [1] in Linlithgowshire, which continued to be the chief seat of the Hospitallers in Scotland until their suppression. King David, in 1153, confirmed by charter the possession and privileges of the Order in Scotland, and succeeding monarchs confirmed and augmented these foundations. Yet in 1338, the year of the report, the property of the Order in Scotland appears to have realized nothing, on account of the long continuance of devastating war. In more peaceful times the revenue appears to have been two hundred marks, or £66 13s. 4d.

In Ireland the Order, almost immediately after the conquest of that country by the English, was represented by a settlement on a site at Kilmainham, where tradition says a church had already stood (the prefix Kil meaning a church), erected by the holy prince Maignend six centuries before. Strongbow's foundation took place in 1174. After the suppression of the Order of the Temple at a later date, and consequently the absorption of their preceptory of Clontarf by the Hospitallers, another extension of the priory buildings took place, a little to the eastward of their original situation: the exact position of the premises as then arranged is per-

[1] "Templaria," Edinburgh, 1828.

KILMAINHAM PRIORY: EAST FRONT.

THE ORDER IN ENGLAND 37

petuated by the east window of the existing chapel left intact at the later seventeenth-century rebuilding. The possessions of the Order in Ireland consisted of twenty-one commanderies, viz.: in the county of Dublin, Kilmainham and Clontarf; in Kildare, Kilbegs, Kilhead and Tully; in Carlow, Killergy; in Meath, Kilmainhambeg and Kilmainhamwood; in Louth, Kilsaran; in Down, Ardes; in Waterford, the four commanderies of Killbarry, Killara, Crook and Nincrioch; in Cork, Morne or Mora; in Tipperary, Clonmel; in Galway, Kinalkin; in Sligo, Teaque Temple, and in Wexford, Kildogan, Ballyhawk and Wexford. General Porter (who supplies this list) adds that there are no records left of the value of this Irish property. However, we may venture to state that the Order had large and thriving estates in all parts of the United Kingdom. Monastic bodies were good landlords, generally speaking, and their tenants were exempt from many duties and services. That the position of the tenants of the Hospital was an enviable one we have evidence in the Act of Parliament passed to prevent the practice of setting up crosses on their lands and houses by occupiers who had not the Order for their landlords, in the hope that they might share these privileges.[1]

Perhaps the best illustration of the mode in which the balance sheet of the English revenue in the fourteenth century is made out will be by taking the

[1] Southey, "Commonplace Book" (vol. i., 464).

38   HOSPITALLERS OF ST. JOHN

accounts of the Bailiwick of Eagle [1] with its members.
Income.

A manor house with garden worth per annum	20 shillings.
Two dovecotes	10 shillings.
Rent of assize—with out-rent	53 marks [2] 17 pence.
Rent of hens	50 shillings.
Works and customs worth	£4 2s. 2d.
Two windmills and one watermill	30 shillings.
Four carucates of land containing 500 acres; and at Wodehouse three carucates containing 300, at 6d. an acre	£20 0s. 0d.
At Wysseby 54 acres at 4d. an acre in all	18 shillings.
At Eycle (Eagle) 50 acres of meadow at 2s. an acre in all	100 shillings.
Of profit of underwood	100 shillings.
Pleas and perquisites of the courts	100 shillings.
The church of Eagle, appropriated, worth	22 marks.
The church of Swynderby, appropriated, worth	22 marks.
Rent of Sybbethorp, worth	10 marks.
Twenty acres of meadow at Wysseby, worth	40 shillings.
Pasture for 20 cows, worth	40 shillings.
Pasture for 400 sheep, worth	33s. 4d.
Sum total of Receipt and Profit of the said Bailiwick	£122 11s. 10d.

" Reprises.

" Out of which in house expenses, viz.: For the Preceptor, one Brother, two Secular Chaplains, Philip de Beverley, Corrodary, Lord Henry de Baneby, Corrodary, Nicholas de Leybourn, Corrodary, Adam de Sprottlee, Corrodary, and others of the household:

[1] Hugo, "History of Eagle."   [2] Mark, value 13s. 4d.

THE ORDER IN ENGLAND 39

In bread yearly, 70 quarters of wheat, at 2s. 6d. a quarter, in all	£8 15s.
In malt beer, 100 quarters of barley malt, at 2s. a quarter	£10.
In flesh, fish and other necessaries for the kitchen, at 4s. a week	£10 4s.
In the provender of the horses of the Preceptor and guests, 182 quarters at 1s. a quarter, in all	£9 2s.
For the sustentation of the houses through the whole Bailiwick	60 shillings.
In rent resolute yearly to divers lords	£1 6s. 8d.
To the Archdeacon of Lincoln, for procurations of the Churches of Eycle and Swynderby	14s. 10d.
To Hugh de Longeton, annual pension for life	8 marks.
To John, Vicar of the Church of Synderby pension for life, by the charter of Br. Thomas Larcher, allowed in the responsions	40 shillings.
To Nicholas de Leybourn, for life, by charter of the same	£1 6s. 8d.
To Philip de Beverley, for life, by charter of the same	13s. 4d.
To John de Weston, for life, by deed of the Temple	4 marks.
In the visitation of the Prior, during two days	40 shillings.
In the stipends of two Chaplains	40 shillings.
In robe, mantle and necessaries of one Brother	£1 14s. 8d.
In robes and wages of one forester, cook, baker, dispenser and one gatekeeper, to each one mark	5 marks.
To laundress	2s.
To two pages, to each three shillings	6 shillings.
Sum total of all expenses and payments.	£55 17s. 4d.
Sum of value. So there remain to be paid to the Treasurer for supporting burdens.	100 marks.

Names of the Brethren :
    Br. Rob. Cort, Preceptor, Knt.
    Br. Joh. de Wytlefford, Chaplain

Corrody—Philip de Beverley, allowed in the
responsions . . . . 10 marks.

"Here then we have a valuable estate with a minute balance sheet of its income and expenditure, the enumeration of its officers, civil and ecclesiastical, its Preceptor, responsible to the Prior of Clerkenwell, as he again was to the Grand Master of the Order, and rendering an exact account of all receipts and outgoings, with the balance which remained for transmission to the common treasury."

Many of the items are of considerable interest even in our own day, as showing how we may arrive at an appreciation of the social life of the fourteenth century, and draw conclusions respecting the most interesting of all conceivable pictures, the history of human daily life in times both earlier and later than those in this plain way recorded for us. As Mr. Kemble truly says: "The fourteenth century did not stand alone or apart: it was the child of the thirteenth and it was also the father of the fifteenth, influenced by the one and influencing the other."

The "works and customs," for example, represent those services which, as before mentioned, were required by right from tenants, and were sometimes commuted for a money payment. The courts were those of the Manor where minor pleas were tried. From the churches served by their vicars the commandery derived a considerable revenue. Eagle itself was worth twenty-two marks, or £14 6s., and if

THE ORDER IN ENGLAND 41

we presume that Hugh de Longeton was vicar, his income in money stands at £5 6s. 8d., while John, vicar of Swynderby, a benefice of similar value, receives but forty shillings a year. The visitation expenses strike one as being disproportionate. The Archdeacon's cost 14s. 10d., while the Prior, whose duty it was to visit every year, had expended on him and his retinue during the two days of his stay the considerable sum of 40s. After all deductions, however, there remained for the common treasury a fair amount of surplus, as money was then estimated, namely, 100 marks, or £66 13s. 4d.

On the side of expenditure the items which demand most notice are those under the head of corrodary or commons, a heavy charge on this as on other manors, and especially felt at headquarters in Clerkenwell. These are no doubt frequently repayments for money lent, or reservations upon estates granted, or even stipulated returns for favours conferred. The corrodary, if gentle, is accommodated at the Preceptor's table, and has the same allowances as a *confrater*, except, in perhaps the robe, mantle, and *necessaria*. Other corrodaries have their commons, according to their rank, with the *liberi servientes* or the *garciones*. And in Clerkenwell there were corrodaries who were more amply and liberally treated than the brethren themselves. Some of these are indeed so instructive that it is worth while to call particular attention to them. In Clerkenwell it is stipulated that William de Langeford is to have his commons with the convent or brotherhood whenever it is his pleasure to dine in hall, and commons for one chamberlain at the table of the free servants, and for two *garciones* (lads) and one *pajettus* at the table of the *garciones*. And if the said William shall please to dine out of hall, he shall receive a fixed allowance of four white loaves, two loaves of ration bread (*panis carpentariorum*), two loaves of black bread, three flagons of the better sort of beer, two flagons of the second sort, and from each service of the kitchen one whole dish, on the same footing as a brother; and for his chamberlain, one whole dish of the sort supplied to the free servants; and for his aforesaid *garciones*, one whole dish of the sort served to the *garciones* : and every night for his chamber, one flagon of the best beer, and, at the season of the year, every night four candles and one faggot of small wood; hay, litter, a shoe and nails, and half a bushel of oats for his horses; and all these things he is to have, at his own will, from day to day for the term of his life, by virtue of the charter of the chapter granted him in the time of brother Thomas L'Archer and brother Leonard de Tybertis.

"Item, Alan Gille takes daily three white loaves, three loaves of ration bread, two black loaves, two flagons of the best beer, and one of the second quality, allowance from the kitchen as for two

THE ORDER IN ENGLAND 43

brothers, or two pence a day for the kitchen;[1] and if there should happen to be pittance,[2] he is to be served at the rate of two brothers, or to have one penny in the name of pittance; and every year, four wain-loads of bush, and seven quarters of charcoal, one wain-load of litter, and four wain-loads of hay; and every night, half a bushel of oats, and candle as much as two brothers have; and when the convent happens to drink wine, he is to have the allowance of two brothers.

"And all this Alan Gille had by virtue of a charter of brother Thomas L'Archer, who, I fear, was an extravagant manager, and had got into the hands of the usurers, Lombards and others, not to say Jews; for even this may be suspected, since I find one Thomas Isaac a corrodary at the brethren's table in Clerkenwell."

But it was not Prior L'Archer only who granted such privileges. A grant quoted from Archdall's "Monasticon" will show them in exercise in Ireland in 1350. "Prior Roger Outlawe[3] granted to Master Walter Islip, during life, entertainment for himself,

---

[1] So one penny a day was the kitchen allowance of a brother of the Order.

[2] If a "feast day."

[3] Outlawe deserves honourable memory for his refusal, when acting as Lord Justice, to entertain a charge of witchcraft preferred by Ledred, Bishop of Ossory, in 1329, against Alice Kettle and her son William. A charge of heresy was thereupon brought against him by the Bishop, but in the sequel, the charge recoiled upon Ledred himself, who was banished from Ireland.

two upper servants, a chamberlain and another servant, five boys and five horses. The said Walter to sit at the right hand of the Prior, thereby to be more commodiously served in eating and drinking. His chaplain to have a place at the table with the brethren of the house. That his pad and other horses should have the same forage with the Prior's. That at the feast of the Nativity, annually, he should have a gown and four garments of the better kind of cloth, the same as the Prior's; his chaplain clothed in like manner as the brethren, and his servants as those of the Prior. That when he dined in his own apartments he should have three white loaves equal in goodness and size to the Prior's; ten flaggons of the best ale; beef, mutton, and pork from the kitchen, raw or dressed as the Prior was served, together with roast meat or soup. That with his servants and goods he should have ingress and egress through all gates and doors belonging to the Priory. That he should have a proper place within the walls of the castle near the great gate to build a stable for his horses, and part of the garden near the said gate to make a nursery. That whenever the said Walter should dine in the hall, or in the Prior's chamber, he should be allowed for his evening potation after dinner, three flaggons of the best ale; and that in the seasons of Lent and other times of fasting he should be served with flesh meat as usual, unless he chose to abstain from it."

THE ORDER IN ENGLAND 45

Over and above the cost of these pensioners of the Order, a vast outlay, totally without return, was occasioned by the public entertainment of wayfarers at the various preceptories. Hospitality was the general rule of the brethren of the Order; impressed upon them, as we find from their charters, both by the donors of estates and by the obligations which they held in common with other monastic orders. When we remember that the first necessity for a poor law in England arose from the suppression of the monasteries dispersed throughout the counties of England and Wales, where a reception had been given to all *supervenientes* (wayfarers), both for horse and man, we see that these houses in fact supplied the right to hospitality enjoyed by the poor, which we have learned nowadays to call relief, and strive more or less successfully to regulate. "But while," says Mr. Kemble, "this perennial claim existed in the fourteenth century, though in different form, it no doubt caused some difficulty to the preceptors and priors who sought to limit it. There would be an anxiety on the part of the administrators lest through laxity they should over-burden their funds, and an equal determination on the part of some of the applicants to get as much as possible out of them. The fourteenth century had its compromises, as the twentieth will have, though they may take different forms; therefore it is clear that the Hospitallers and their guests must have acted reciprocally upon an understanding that there was a limit somewhere or other to what the house had to supply, and the guest had a right to receive. There must have been a distinction between guest and guest; and, above all, there must have been a settled rule as to the time during which a stranger could claim a share in the abundance of the house. In this respect it is to be presumed that the rule of all monastic houses applied to the Hospitallers, who were in part at least a monastic order. Now I believe (says Mr. Kemble) that, almost universally (except, indeed, where sickness gave a claim to tendance in the infirmary, where such existed for strangers), the limit of claim in monasteries was three days. This is strictly consonant with the ancient universal Teutonic law, which looks upon a man for three days as a guest in a house, but after that time as a member of the family, for whom the householder had to account. "Three days *gast*," says the Anglo-Saxon law: "after that *agen hins*," your own domestic. And so the German proverb said, "A three nights' guest stinks," *i.e.*, approaches the time when it is necessary to turn him out, unless you mean to assume all the responsibility of providing for and representing him. The three days seem also to have been the rule upon the Continent, and it may be therefore presumed to have been universally adopted from the earliest periods in all Christian communities. Accordingly it is to be imagined that a single person might in strict law claim food and

THE ORDER IN ENGLAND 47

lodging for three days in a preceptory, which would be supplied as befitting his condition; but that strict law was not likely to be very closely followed. It is more likely that the "Family" would do pretty much as they liked about guests of a certain sort; not perhaps refusing relief, but taking care that it should not be so given as to render a second application very probable. They may possibly have had their equivalents for the crank and the stone heap. At the open table of the *liberi servientes* or *garciones* a good fellow might, and perhaps often did, make himself welcome, and no one would ask him how long he had stayed or meant to stay. On the other hand, the knight or esquire, who had something to tell or something to give, might extend his visit to the great satisfaction of the preceptor and confrater. And then let us remember what this hospitality brought in. How great a thing it was to gather round one men from all parts of the country, or from foreign countries; to collect information which in those days no daily paper detailed over the breakfast table; to hear news, learn prices, compare information, and instruct the heads of the Order. Was not hospitality —regulated, if one found it troublesome, unlimited, if one liked it—a noble, charitable, Christian, and— profitable virtue? How many valuable hints, may we imagine, were sent up from Chippenham, or Dynmore, or Trebigh to Clerkenwell, there to be carefully compared with other information from

Greenham, and Southampton, and Sutton at Hone? How many reports thereupon despatched to Rhodes? How many instructions thence issued to the four quarters of the globe? The newspaper tells us what is doing, but it tells our neighbours as soon, and in as much detail. Here information was gathered which none else could gather, and a perfect network spread all over Europe, of which the main thread was in one hand. It was worth the expenditure in bread, and beeves, and beer, we may be sure.

Such were the principal items of income and expenditure which appear in all the various Commanderies as recorded in this valuable document. From it we also learn that there were 116 brethren of the Order at that time residing in England, in addition to 80 corrodaries and 3 donats. These latter were persons who, though not professed members of the fraternity, were affiliated thereto and derived sundry privileges therefrom, owing to their having made donations to the funds of the Order.

Of the 116 brethren 34 were Knights of Justice, 34 were Chaplains, and 48 were Serving Brothers. There were 36 Commanderies, the Commanders over which were in 13 cases Knights, in 7 they were Chaplains, and in 16 they were Serving Brothers.

The Order of St. John, from its social and political standing, was exposed, no doubt, to calls from which other convents were free. A large expense at

Monument of Sir William Weston,
Lord Prior of the O.S.J.I. in England: ob: A.D. 1540

THE ORDER IN ENGLAND 49

Hampton is explained: "Because the Duke of Cornwall was staying in the neighbourhood." On the marches of Wales a constantly moving and restless population were not less troublesome; great are the complaints of Welsh tramps in the preceptories of Dinmore (Herefordshire) and Slebach (Pembroke); the preceptor in the latter case denouncing them as "great wasters and mighty burdensome."

The proximity of Clerkenwell to London and Westminster particularly exposed it to this sort of inconvenience. As a matter of course, every brother from the country who had business in London took up his quarters with the Prior: "I should think," says Mr. Kemble once more, "that Chief Justice Scrope dined there very often, especially while the litigation about the Temple estates was going on. It must have been good and grave fun in its way, when the King's Bench and Common Pleas, the Exchequer and Chancery, and Privy Council met together over the hospitable board of Clerkenwell, and speculated whether the noble keep of Temple Bruere, or the rich manor of Temple Cowley, would help to mend the next feast-day; or whether it was very likely that Ralph Nevill would be squeezed into giving up Faxfleet; or Stroud would get out of the hands of the Countess of Pembroke; or Earl Warenne would be content to relinquish Saddlccomb, with its comfortable little revenue

E

of sixty-six pounds, eight shillings, per annum. But it was all mighty good company, and the Prior of Clerkenwell sighs out his complaint in a gentle tone."

For which burthens four hundred and thirty quarters of corn, etc., were needed. Poor Hospitallers of Clerkenwell, and poor Grand Master in Rhodes! It was truly hard that that milch-cow of the Continent, England, should not give every drop that could be got by squeezing, even though her own calves might die in the midst of plenty. Many of the distinguished guests of the Prior were lodged in the gate-house at Clerkenwell. The business of the great ambulance work of to-day may be actually proceeding in apartments where L'Isle Adam stayed on his memorable visit to King Henry VIII., and where most of the home concerns of the English Langue with their tenants or dependants were transacted. The building which exists at present replaced the original gate-house destroyed by Wat Tyler's mob in 1381, and was not finished until 1504 by Prior Thomas Dowcra, last but one of the English Grand Priors. The list of these dignitaries commences with a Neapolitan, for (as has been noted before) the spirit of the Order was cosmopolitan, nor is it until the fourth Prior, Alban, who in 1195 became Bishop of Bangor, that we have an Englishman of note in the post. Gilbert de Vere comes next, and native names are frequent in the

THE ORDER IN ENGLAND 51

twelve successors who bring us down to the date of Thomas L'Archer, already spoken of. Whether this Prior were an incapable or an unfortunate administrator may be a moot point: at any rate he fell upon evil days, for the headquarters of the Order were rent by schism and disputed election of a Grand Master, while in England so great was the confusion in the affairs of the Hospital, that the first act of the Grand Master Elyan de Villeneuf, when his unanimous election restored harmony at Rhodes in 1328, was to despatch Leonard de Tybertis, Prior of Venice, as his vicar or representative. On his arrival he found the ruin of the fraternity nearly complete; the Lombards and Perugians, to whom the convent owed money, being as relentless creditors as if they had been Turks themselves. The first thing Leonard de Tybertis did was to meet the most urgent and pressing demands of the creditors by part payments and by undertakings on the faith of which the writs were withdrawn for the present. Thomas L'Archer was suspended or deposed, and Leonard de Tybertis elected *ad interim*. By his influence and judicious outlay, partly also it should seem by the mortgage of his costly jewels, he succeeded in raising no less a sum than two thousand three hundred and thirty-seven pounds, eleven shillings and fourpence on loan, which, with the regular income of the Priory, sufficed to pay off the most pressing burthens, and to give the Order some breathing time; and the English brethren, grateful for his aid, and perhaps desirous of the continuance of his beneficial intervention, solicited from the Grand Master his confirmation as Prior of England. It is said in general that the estates of the Templars only came into the hands of the Priory during the priorate of Leonard; but even from this letter, in which the confirmation of his election is desired, it is clear that the brotherhood already held Temple lands, which produced in the year 1328 four hundred and fifty-eight pounds, one shilling and ten pence. Still, we may infer from the universal tradition that he was very active in the affair of the transfer; and in all probability it was not more his skill in reducing the debts than his success in obtaining seisin of the Temple estates which were yet withheld, that induced the English preceptors to make him their Prior. But it is certain that even ten years later some of the most valuable of the Temple manors had not been surrendered to the Hospital; and it is well known that some never were. The litigation consequent upon these various complications explains, though it does not excuse, the sums paid to the judges and other influential members of the King's Council of State.[1]

---

[1] It is very significant that, among the sums raised to meet the immediate difficulty, we find as much as £202 10s. reckoned as well or profitably earned by "Corrodies."

In looking over the list of pensions granted previously to and

THE ORDER IN ENGLAND 53

It is very possible that Thomas L'Archer was rather an unfortunate than an incapable administrator. It is certain that Leonard de Tybertis raised money in the same way, receiving capital in hand, and giving estates at low rents, or settling, as above said, corrodies and rent-charges upon particular manors. Leases for life,[1] or term of years,[2] were granted in this manner; and, although the interest was usurious, and, according to the doctrine then prevalent, utterly illegal, it was impossible for the English Priory to save itself on any other terms. The skill with which a prior could raise money under such circumstances — in other words, the cheaper he could get it in the long run—was the real measure of his capacity, and possibly if Thomas L'Archer were deposed, it was quite right that he should be so. He was an unlucky Chancellor of the Exchequer, for whom there is no mercy. Leonard accounted for in 1338, we find sums cited to the following amounts under various Priors:

	£	s.	d.
Under J. Chauncy	1	0	0
W. de Tothall	3	6	8
A. Montague	10	0	0
R. Paveley	5	0	0
T. L'Archer	233	6	8
Leonard de Tybertis	82	12	0

[1] "Ewell, in Kent."
[2] *Vide* "Marnham," p. 161; "Kelyngton," p. 143 (Kemble). It is to be regretted that churches should so often have been bought and sold in this money-raising transaction.

de Tybertis acted upon the same principle, but applied it with more discretion; and he lived a respected man, and died Prior of England.[1]

[1] Kemble.

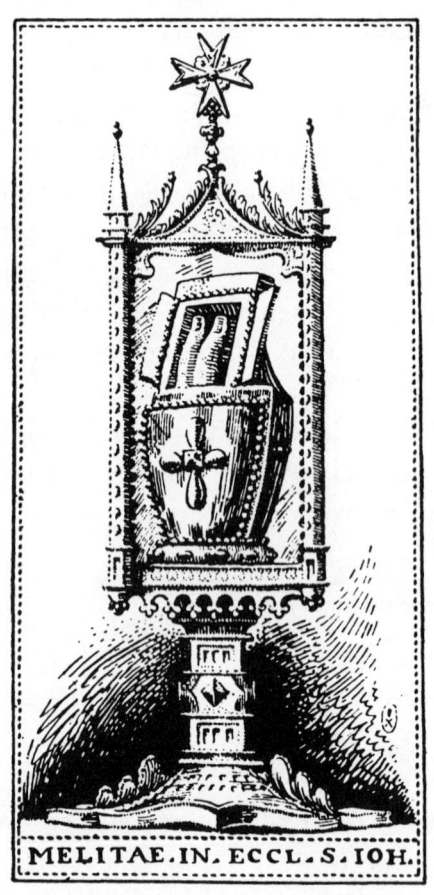

HAND OF ST. JOHN IN ITS ORIGINAL CASE
From an engraving of 1755

CHAPTER IV

THE ORDER IN ENGLAND (*continued*)

THE original glories of the Priory in Clerkenwell have so completely passed away, that it is difficult even in imagination to restore them. The buildings and their gardens covered a space of full five acres, from the site of the present gate-house down to the River of Wells, which then sparkled and rippled along the Fleet valley fed by multitudinous springs on either bank.

The present Gate [1] is not one of the original buildings of the Priory, all that was above ground having been destroyed during the great popular outbreak of 1381, when Jack Straw, on June 13th, led a furious multitude to the destruction of the Priory and the "ruination" of the dwelling at Highbury of the unpopular Prior, Sir Robert Hales, Lord High Treasurer of England in Richard II.'s minority. The Prior himself was beheaded on Tower Hill at the same time as Simon Sudbury, Archbishop of Canterbury, and others. The rebuilding of the Priory was soon commenced, but the Gate, which was the last part of

---

[1] "Architectural Notice of St. John's Gate," by W. Griffith, 1870.

the building to be finished, was not completed until 1504, as appears by the date placed thereon with his arms by Prior Docwra. It is probable, from the appearance of the work, that it is entirely of the Tudor period, replacing perhaps a temporary entrance erected at the end of the fourteenth century. The foundations of the existing towers are, however, those of the original gate-house. Docwra's work consists of walls three feet thick of brickwork faced with Ryegate stone. On the north and south fronts of the existing archway are projecting towers; in the western tower the old spiral staircase still remains in use. The Tudor-headed doorways are also intact, and one oak carving bears the arms of the Priory and of Docwra. In each angle of the gateway is a slender shaft attached to the wall with a well-moulded base and capital. From these spring the ribs which support the groined vault, ornamented with sculptured bosses and shields.[1]

We may form a general idea of the premises from a request to purchase, by Viscount Lisle, after the suppression. The Gate-house is specially mentioned, being described as covered with lead; three gardens are also stated to have been attached to it, and an orchard, with a fishpond to the east and north. Next came the sub-priors' lodging with gardens, the Turcopolier's house and garden, the great and little courts, the wood-house and yard, the slaughter-house, the

[1] Hugo, "St. John's Gate," 1875.

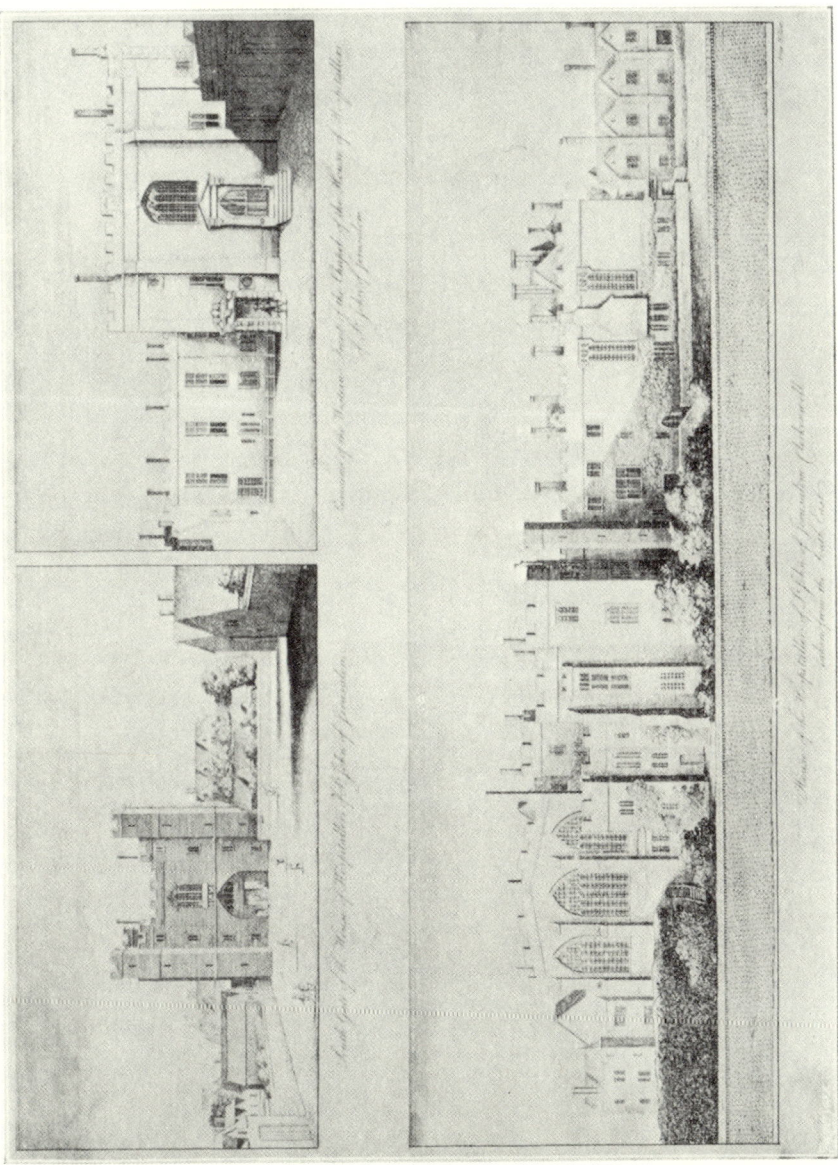

THE ORDER IN ENGLAND

plumber's house, the laundry, the counting-house, etc., etc., also all the boundary walls of the premises. Here might have been mentioned the church with its superb bell-tower, the glory of the north-west of London, "a most curious piece of workmanship," says Stowe; but in 1548 Protector Somerset used his tutorial privilege during the minority of King Edward VI., to destroy the Great Bell Tower for its materials, which he used for his new mansion in the Strand. It was barbarously, says the chronicler, "undermined and blown up with gunpowder," so that only part of the choir survived this destruction. That portion of the church was closed up at the west end, and repaired by Cardinal Pole in Queen Mary's reign, but after the second confiscation of the funds of the Order also fell into decay, until restored in a measure to sacred uses by Simon Michell in 1721, when it was converted into a parish church, being sold to the Commissioners appointed under an act of Queen Anne for building fifty new churches in London. Much has been lately done to improve the building, but little of the old work remains above ground, save the east windows of Prior Docwra's time, the south wall, and the bases of the original columns, traceable between the seats of the modern structure. In the centre east window is a small shield of arms of stained glass, inscribed "Robertus Botyll, Pryor. Elect A.D., 1439. Resig. 1469." It is believed that the Earl of Aylesbury, during the seventeenth century, resided in the house adjoining, and used the choir as his private chapel. During the Sacheverell riots it is supposed to have become a Dissenters' meeting-house, as Burnet, Bishop of Salisbury, who lived in St. John's Square, describes an attack by the mob upon "a meeting-house near me, out of which they drew everything that was in it, and burned it before the door of the house."

The crypt, which, during the eighteenth and nineteenth centuries was choked with human remains and decomposing coffins, has been of late years under thorough and judicious restoration, and it is now, as it ought to be, one of the best preserved relics of old London.

It now remains to give a brief chronicle of the downfall of the Order. On the adoption by Henry VIII. of the measure for suppressing the monasteries, the Priory of St. John was too important to be left out, though its position was in some degree different from that of other convents. Henry was reported in 1527 to have entertained the idea of appointing a favourite of his own as Prior, and of separating the English Langue from the rest of the Order, stationing the knights at Calais. The personal intercession of G. M. de L'Isle Adam is said to have prevented this. It is possible that Henry entertained the idea of an English Order with the King instead of the Grand Master at its head; certainly the letters patent bearing date at Westminster, 7th July, 1538

THE CRYPT, NORTH TRANSEPT.
Before the removal of the human remains.

THE NAVE OF THE CRYPT, FROM THE WEST DOOR.
ST. JOHN'S CHURCH, CLERKENWELL.

THE ORDER IN ENGLAND 59

(of which the original is still in the archives at Malta, while the library at St. John's Gate has a certified copy), certainly do no more than substitute the King for the Grand Master, by requiring the oath of allegiance as a condition of the tenure of English lands by the Priory. The original document, handsomely adorned with a portrait of Henry and heraldic devices, is thus summarized by General Porter: "The document bears date 7th July, 1538, and commences by entitling Henry VIII. the supreme head of the Anglican Church, and as such the protector of the Order of St. John of Jerusalem in England. It then goes on to declare, first, that for himself and his successors he gives licence to Brother William West (Weston), Grand Prior of England, to confer the habit and receive the profession requisite to admit such English subjects as may desire to enter the Order, under the usual conditions, provided that such postulant shall have previously taken an oath of allegiance to the said monarch: secondly, that any person nominated by the Grand Master in Council to a commandery in England shall obtain confirmation of his appointment from the King; he will be required to pay the first year's revenue of his commandery into the King's treasury: thirdly, it shall not be lawful for the Order of St. John to make eleemosynary collections within the realm of England unless in virtue of a Royal warrant, which warrant shall contain the express clause that such collection was not made in virtue of any bull from the Roman Pontiff, but under letters patent emanating from the King of England (these collections had hitherto been frequently made under the sanction of Papal authority, and formed a considerable source of revenue under the title of Confraria) : fourthly, those brethren holding or hereafter promoted to commanderies within the realm of England, shall not recognize, support or promote the jurisdiction, authority, rank, or title of the Bishop of Rome : fifthly, those brethren holding or hereafter promoted to commanderies within the realm of England, shall after the payment of the first year's revenues into the King's treasury, transfer those of the second year to the treasury of the Order for the general maintenance and support of the convent with the reservation of such annual tithes as the King retains to himself from all the commanderies within the kingdom : sixthly, and lastly, that every year a chapter of the Priory shall be held, in which all crimes committed by the fraternity within the realm of England shall be examined into and duly punished ; and if any of the offending brethren shall consider himself aggrieved by the sentence of the Chapter, he shall appeal either to the vicar of the King, or to the conservator of the privileges of the Order of St. John duly appointed by the King."

It may be argued that these terms might have been accepted by any body of men without discredit, and that the fidelity of the Knights of St. John was some-

THE ORDER IN ENGLAND 61

what quixotic when they lost the opportunity of a national sanction of Hospitaller work by their adherence to the constitution to which they had vowed allegiance. Yet, judging from the events of Henry's reign, and from the fact that after the loss of Rhodes he had been with difficulty persuaded not to lay hands upon the property of the Order, we need not hesitate to say that the rapacity of the Court would have eventually absorbed the commanderies, and certainly the reproach which attended the surrender of Malta two hundred and fifty years later would have attached to the English branch, which the Italian Bosio has thus eulogized : "*cosi ricco nobile e principal membro arme sampra era stata la venerabile lingua d'Inghilterra.*"

True it was that in consequence of their fidelity not only did a general sequestration of their property take place in England, but that many of their members suffered for their opposition to the autocratic will of Henry, while others, exiles or banished, resorted to the headquarters of the Order. Allowances were promised to certain of the retiring knights, commencing with a pension of £1,000 a year to the Prior, Sir W. Weston. But as that faithful soul did not survive even by a day the dissolution of his Priory, we know that he received nothing of the price granted to him. He died 7th May, 1540, the same day on which the Priory was dissolved. Of the members of the Order, Sir Thomas Dingley, Sir

Marmaduke Bowes, and Sir Adrian Fortescue were attainted together of high treason for denying the King's supremacy on the 20th April, 1539, and were all beheaded. Sir David German, for the same reason, was condemned to death, and having been drawn in a sledge through Southwark was hanged and quartered at St. Thomas Watering on July 1st, 1541.

The possessions of the Order and its commanderies were thus transferred to the Crown and its nominees. The deer park between Paddington and Hampstead with the adjacent Priory of Kilburn (forty-six acres), formerly the seat of an independent convent, but since the expulsion of the nuns in 1536 the property of the Order, were a portion of the spoil and retain the name of St. John's Wood.

The ladies of Buckland also had to leave their convent. They were granted pensions of small amount, but there is much reason to fear that many of these were never paid.

It is noteworthy that Stow records "the priory church and house of St. John were preserved from spoil or pulling down so long as Henry VIII. reigned, and were employed as a store house for the king's toils and tents for hunting and for the wars." Edward VI. on his accession granted to his sister the Princess Mary, by letters patent, the site, circuit, ambit, precinct, capital, messuage, and house late of the Priory of St. John of Jerusalem at Clerkenwell.

THE ORDER IN ENGLAND 63

Despite the grant, and we may be pretty sure against the Princess's wish, the church was ruthlessly pulled down the following year. When Mary succeeded her half-brother, Royal letters patent were issued on April 2nd, 1557, incorporating the bailiffs, commanders, and knights of St. John, by and under the name and title of the Prior and co-brethren of the Hospital of St. John of Jerusalem in England, giving them as a corporation a common seal, and ordaining for the Crown, its heirs and successors, that the knights of the Order in England should for ever have and enjoy their name, style and dignity, with all their ancient privileges and prerogatives. Sir Thomas Tresham was appointed Grand Master of the English Convent.

In the archives of Malta is a deed of Philip and Mary, dated 1554, re-endowing and re-establishing the Order in Ireland; but one of the earliest acts of Queen Elizabeth annexed to the Crown all its possessions within the kingdom, without, however, enacting the dissolution of the corporate body established by the charter of Mary.

It is remarkable that neither at this period nor at the former dissolution did any very large proportion of the members of the fraternity of the Hospital in England resort to Malta. Only two English names, Shelley and Starkey, occur at the date of the famous siege, and the very modest dimensions of the Auberge d'Angleterre, erected near the Porto Reale in the new city of Valletta, indicate an idea that the Langue would never regain any considerable dimensions : although through its later history the Grand Masters exhibited a certain care to keep an open door for revival. The Grand Master himself appropriated the title of Turcopolier *in commendam*, thus avoiding the necessity of another appointment ; and when, a century later, there seemed some probability of attracting the English Jacobites, James Fitzjames, Duke of Berwick, was proclaimed head of the English Langue, but with no apparent result in bringing adherents to its ranks. After Grand Master de Rohan had requested George III.'s consent to the use of the name "Anglo-Bavarian" for the new Langue which he proposed to found, more friendly relations began to prevail, and a few English Protestants, chiefly officers in the navy, were honoured with the cross of the Order by Grand Master Hompesch ; but in England its distinctions came to be regarded more and more as secular honours conferred by a foreign potentate.

It is singular, however, that Elizabeth, although she annexed the possessions of the Order, extended a sort of patronage to it. In 1565 public prayers were offered in the diocese of Salisbury (then held by Bishop Jewel) for the deliverance of Malta from the Turks. Upon receipt of the tidings of the abandonment of the siege, a general thanksgiving was ordered throughout the province of Canterbury

THE ORDER IN ENGLAND 65

by Archbishop Parker.[1] In one of the Latin narratives of the war, published in 1596, the author (Caelius Secundus Curio) prefixes to his history a dedication in verse to Queen Elizabeth, whom he highly eulogizes for her goodwill to the Knights of St. John.

The fortunes of the Irish Priory of Kilmainham had become unsettled as far back as the middle of the fifteenth century, when Thomas Fitzgerald, a scion of the powerful Geraldine family, had been removed from his Office as Prior for maladministration. He probably anticipated that by the influence of his connections he might be reinstated, for he retained his official seal, which he used for his own purposes. He did subsequently succeed in recovering his position. A later Prior, James Keating, outdid all his predecessors in audacity and aggrandizement. He fortified the Castle of Dublin against the Royal Deputy, and even when, in 1482, the Grand Master had deposed him from his office by mandate from Rhodes and sent as his successor Marmaduke Lumley, Keating contumaciously defied his authority, held his post, and cast his rival into prison. Ultimately he brought about his own ruin by his support of the claims of Lambert Simnell, the pretended Duke of York, and finally, in 1491, was ejected from his priory. These untoward circumstances facilitated

---

[1] "Liturgies and Services of the Reign of Queen Elizabeth," Parker Society, 1847.

66 HOSPITALLERS OF ST. JOHN

the annexation of the Priory to the Crown. Sir John Rawson (Prior until his death in 1547) was created Lord Clontarf, with a pension to maintain the dignity of a viscount. Oswald Massingberd was nominated at Malta as his successor, but took no steps to assume the dignity until Queen Mary, in 1554, reconstituted the Priory. In the second year of Elizabeth he brought his brief term of office to a close, and half a century later the keeper appointed by Government resigned his post, the buildings having become too ruinous for further occupation. Thus they lay desolate until, in 1679, the Duke of Ormond obtained from Charles II. authority to erect a hospital of the same description as the one at Chelsea, and the east window of the chapel, dedicated anew to the memory of King Charles the Martyr, is the sole surviving remnant of the ancient Priory buildings.

In 1687 Tyrconnel, Lord Deputy, became the Master of the hospital, and has been credited with a design "at some favourable juncture[1] to restore it to the Knights of St. John." In 1688 he inducted an Order of Friars into rooms adjoining the chapel, and gave them charge of it. The Registrar then fled, taking with him the Charter and other documents. In 1690, after the battle of the Boyne, the sick and wounded of King William's army were accommodated in the hospital, and in 1692 the board

[1] Burton's "History of Kilmainham Priory."

TORPHICHEN PRECEPTORY.

THE ORDER IN ENGLAND 67

of governors was again assembled and the constitution of 1679 revived.

Since 1775 the office of Master of the hospital has been attached to the Command-in-Chief of Ireland. The present representative of the Prior of Kilmainham is therefore our Bailiff of Eagle, H.R.H. the Duke of Connaught.

The Preceptory of Torphichen, chief seat of the Order in Scotland, was in 1547 surrendered by the Prior of Scotland, Sir James Sandilands of Calder, into the hands of the Government, and he was created Lord Torphichen. The "Templar Lands" in Edinburgh (mentioned by Scott in the "Heart of Midlothian") were part of the property of this Priory, and during the Scottish wars the Lord of St. John, as the Preceptor was styled, seems often to have been a prominent personage. The last Preceptor, David Seton, retired to Germany, where he died in 1591.

In an old Scottish poem of the latter half of the sixteenth century, entitled "The Holy Kirk and the Theeves," he is mentioned as the head of the Scottish hospitallers. The poem runs thus:

> Fye upon the traitor then,
> Quha has broucht us to sic pass,
> Greedie als the knave Judas;
> Fye upon the churle quwhat solde
> Holie Erthe for heavie golde;
> But the Order felt na losse,
> Quhan David Setonne bare the Crosse.

CHAPTER V

MALTA AND THE GREAT SIEGE

THE Grand Master de L'Isle Adam, after his vain attempts to procure means for the recapture of Rhodes, accepted from the Emperor Charles V. the sovereignty of Malta, to which the knights repaired in October, 1530.

Unattractive as was their new possession by contrast with the verdant fertility of Rhodes, they found one great advantage in the splendid harbours of the northern shore, where the Norman Count, Roger of Sicily, had erected a castle, called St. Angelo. Within this fort, and in the town behind it, they fixed their future capital. They immediately commenced works to enlarge and strengthen the existing fortifications of the promontory on which the castle stood, especially at the point where it touched the mainland. The Grand Masters who succeeded to De L'Isle Adam were constantly employed in this work, and one of them, La Sangle, extended his redoubts to the adjacent promontory then known as St. Julian, since as Senglea.

This improving state of the convent was disturbed by a furious hurricane in 1555—23rd September—

MALTA AND THE GREAT SIEGE 69

which, besides inflicting great damage on shore, wrecked nearly the whole fleet of galleys belonging to the knights; a calamity which encouraged the corsair Dragut, the lieutenant and successor of Barbarossa, to make an attack on the island; but though he ravaged Gozo, and invested the ancient capital of Malta itself, he had to re-embark without accomplishing anything of importance. There can be little doubt that this reconnaissance on his part was the immediate cause of the subsequent siege, for he persuaded the Sultan Solyman that it only required a sufficiently large force to crush this nest of enemies, whose galleys had recently taken the richly-laden ship belonging to the ladies of the seraglio. War was determined upon early in 1565.

For the history which follows, we may rely chiefly upon the narrative of John Anthony Viperan, published at Perugia in 1567. This knight, a member of the Italian Langue, was one of the garrison of the city Notabile during the period of the siege. He afterwards became a bishop in Italy.

The Turkish fleet consisted of 130 galleys and 50 smaller vessels, on board of which were 5,000 Janissaries, 6,000 Spahis, 6,000 Anatolian archers, and 22,000 other soldiers, some armed with muskets, and a large supply of ordnance of a great bulk, and ammunition.

To meet this enormous force, and to garrison the two peninsulas of St. Angelo and Senglea, the fort of St. Elmo, and the detached posts of Notabile and Gozo, the Grand Master, John Parisot la Vallette, who had succeeded to La Sangle in 1555, had a force of rather less than 9,000 men; of these, 474 were knights, and 67 servants at arms, 1,230 regular soldiers, mainly Spanish, 875 volunteers from Italy, and 5,300 of the islanders, a *levy en masse* without much training or special warlike knowledge, though hardy and active, who, in the sequel, by their valour and endurance, proved worthy comrades; and last of all, 700 men released from the galleys, as a desperate resource, to augment the defending strength.

The Turkish force had two commanders, the Admiral Piali, and Mustapha, a veteran general of high repute. They were both enjoined to consult Dragut in any operations which they undertook; but the redoubted corsair had not arrived on May 18th, when they landed their troops at Marsa Scirocco. A difference of opinion thereupon arose (the first of a long series) between the Moslem commanders, Piali proposing that no active operations should be commenced until Dragut's arrival, while Mustapha argued that the possession of St. Elmo was essential to the safety of the fleet. This latter opinion prevailed, and after a couple of ineffectual skirmishes and a threatened attack on Notabile, which was abandoned precipitately, the Turks turned their whole force against St. Elmo.

MALTA AND THE GREAT SIEGE 71

On the 24th of May, the Turkish artillery—18 guns, 10 of which discharged 80lb. shot, and one 160lb.—opened fire upon St. Elmo from the rocky promontory of Mount Schebarras, where it was impossible to trench the soil, so that the besiegers had to form artificial breast-works. It took no long time to pulverize the walls of the fort with the huge cannon-balls of iron and stone which were discharged against it; but as the greater part of the defences were excavated in the live rock, the garrison still had shelter. There was also a passage down to the grand harbour, by which they could communicate with and be reinforced from St. Angelo, for the Turks were so cautious as to confine their batteries to the western side of the eminence, where the crest of the ridge sheltered them from the fire of the castle. A proposal that the fort should be abandoned had been sternly rejected by the Grand Master, who stated that he was willing himself to take the command there rather than that it should not be held to the bitter end. To this purpose he augmented the garrison by 50 knights and 200 Spanish soldiers under Gonzales de Medrano.

The besiegers were at this juncture much strengthened by the arrival of Dragut, who not only brought thirteen ships and 1,500 men, but valuable counsel for the direction of operations. He pointed out the mistake which had been committed by their neglect to occupy Gozo and Notabile, though the reduction of

St. Elmo once having been commenced, he now recommended that it should be persevered with. He erected a battery on the point opposite to the fort on the Sliema side, known by his name until, two centuries later, the French engineer Tigne built a fort there. A sortie under Medrano inflicted great damage on the besiegers' works, but led to the loss of the covered way to the fort; and not long afterwards the Turks surprised and occupied the outwork on the western side. Thus by the 13th June the fort was completely exposed to fire. The enemy's ships also were brought round to the entrance of the harbour to support the attack, and boats were stationed in Renella Bay. Once more three commissioners were sent by La Vallette to report upon the possibility of further defence, two of whom reported the post untenable; but the third offering still to endeavour to defend it, volunteers pressed forward to support the forlorn hope, fresh reinforcements were sent, and a struggle to the death was determined upon. The enemy attacked in force upon the 16th June; and while the main breach in the front of the fort was stormed by 4,000 men, the two flanks were also assailed by means of scaling ladders. After a desperate struggle of six hours' duration, the enemy were repulsed by the garrison at every point, though with the loss of 300 soldiers and seventeen knights, of whom Medrano was one. When night set in, the wounded were removed by

MALTA AND THE GREAT SIEGE 73

boats, and their places taken by fresh volunteers from St. Angelo.

Dragut now insisted upon the necessity of cutting off this communication, and the next few days were spent in placing two cannon in such a position as to command the secret passage. While superintending this work, exposed to the fire from St. Angelo, the corsair was struck upon the head by a fragment of rock, and removed in a dying state to his tent at Tigne.

For three days following the defenders of St. Elmo were exposed to the full fire of the enemy's ordnance, numbering thirty-six pieces. On the 23rd June another general attack was made and repulsed; but the garrison was now reduced to sixty men, who, by an expert swimmer, communicated with La Vallette. He sent boats to bring them off, but his efforts were frustrated by the guns which swept the landing place. All human aid being thus denied them, the defenders sought the last consolations of religion in the little chapel still existing beneath the ramparts, and then took their post, sword in hand, at the top of the breach; some crippled by wounds being supported on seats, to sell their lives as dearly as they could. The first assault of the Turks, incredible as it may sound, was successfully resisted; but renewed hordes of the enemy swarmed in upon them from every side, and scarcely a single Christian survived. Some of the native soldiers, expert swimmers, threw themselves into the water, but only one or two escaped the enemies' boats. When the bodies of those who were lying in the breach were examined, it was found that in nine of them life was not extinct, and these were pounced upon by Dragut's men as available merchandise.

Mustapha took a barbarous revenge upon the lifeless corpses of the knights, which, after decapitation, he tied to planks and set floating in the harbour to be washed past St. Angelo. La Vallette retorted by beheading certain captives, and fired their bleeding heads at the Turks from his cannon.

At this moment Dragut expired.

The Turkish fleet at once occupied the Marsa Muscetto harbour in full force, fifty ships having recently joined them with supplies; moreover, the crews and slaves conveyed some of the lighter vessels across the narrow neck between the Pieta creek and the upper portion of the Grand Harbour, where they launched them so as to attack St. Angelo and St. Michael from the landward side. The entrance to the Grand Harbour was closed by a chain, so fearful were the Turkish commanders of a surprise from Sicily, and, collecting every available soldier, Mustapha invested the two promontories closely, forming a fortified camp where the Cottonera lines now stand. Fortunately for the garrison, on June 29th, just before this investment had been completed, a detachment of their friends from Sicily

SIEGE OF MALTA.
From frescoes in the Palace.

MALTA AND THE GREAT SIEGE 75

added nearly 750 men, forty-two of whom were knights, to the strength of the garrison.

The Turkish commander now sent a flag of truce, with an envoy, to propose terms of surrender to La Vallette. As might be surmised, his real object was, if possible, to detach the natives from their fidelity to the Order by promises of kind treatment in case of surrender. To this message the Grand Master simply returned a stern defiance, and a threat to hang the messenger. No compromise, he declared, was possible. Valuable information as to resources and intentions of the besiegers was obtained in the meantime from a Greek deserter of princely descent, named Lascaris, who contrived to escape from their camp. He rendered important service to the Order in this and other ways. One of his descendants in the next century entered the Order and became Grand Master.

July had now set in with excessive heat, and the Turkish commanders determined upon a grand attack, chiefly directed against a stockade which, at Lascaris's suggestion, had been erected about six yards from the shore along the Corradino face of the promontory of Senglea. Hassan of Algiers had just arrived in the Turkish camp with twenty-seven ships and 2,500 men, and to him the assault was intrusted on July 15th. He commanded on land, while his lieutenant, Candelissa, led the attack by water, selecting, says Viperan, men who did not know how to swim, that they might fight more desperately on landing. He also made his boats stand off, as soon as they had disembarked in water which reached shoulder high. They carried the stockade, and, an explosion having thrown the defenders of the breach into confusion, were on the point of scaling that also, had not Zanoguerra, the Spanish commander, with desperate energy fought them step by step. Mustapha had embarked 1,000 of his choicest Janissaries in ten large barges, and despatched them to attack the point of Isola. In doing this they exposed themselves to the fire of a battery at the water's edge of St. Angelo, and the effect of the volley was to sink nine of the ten boats, with the loss of at least half the attacking force. At the same time a column from the Borgo came across the bridge of boats to the assistance of the defenders of Senglea, and both Hassan and Candelissa were routed with great slaughter, no quarter being given, and the boats having to return some distance to rescue the fugitives. The loss of this memorable day to the Turks was nearly 3,000, and 250 of the garrison fell, including the commandant, Zanoguerra, and the son of the Viceroy of Sicily.

No other serious attempt at assault by boats was made after this; Candelissa being stationed at the mouth of the harbour to intercept any relieving fleet, and a squadron cruising off Syracuse for the same purpose under a corsair named Cavagiali.

MALTA AND THE GREAT SIEGE 77

On the 2nd August, Mustapha made a great effort on St. Michael's fort without any better success than Hassan, a mine which he had intended to spring upon the defenders having been exploded by them during its construction.

The error of leaving Notabile unmolested was now practically evidenced; every day 100 or 150 horsemen left that city and repaired to Casals Zabbar, Zebbug, or Tarschien, to harass the rear of the Turkish army. On the 7th August another assault in force having been delivered upon both promontories, the bastions of Castile and St. Michael's were simultaneously assailed, and while Piali was repulsed with great loss in the first, the latter all but fell into the hands of Mustapha, who had planted on the fort the Turkish standards, when he suddenly gave the signal for retreat. The cause of this was that the contingent from Notabile, having found (so Viperan tells us) a secret path from Tarschien to a spot within a dart's cast of the Turkish camp, surprised and cut down the guards, and were slaughtering the sick and plundering the tents there. Of course the alarm spread that the relieving army had landed, and the Turks hastened back. On the 18th August, Piali contrived by means of a mine to breach the Castile bastion to such an extent that, Viperan says, a horseman could easily have surmounted the wide and easy incline; but La Vallette's firmness prevented any decisive advantage from this success, though for four days every effort was exerted to make good a footing in the defences. The Grand Master himself took up his quarters close to the breach to encourage his followers.

Great use was made here, as at St. Elmo, of fireballs, fireworks, pots of earthenware full of wildfire (saltpetre, camphor, varnish, and pitch), hollow cylinders of wood filled with the same combination, and a hoop surrounded with flax steeped in inflammable matter. Often when these missiles were thrown on the Christian squadrons, the armour they wore rendered it a comparatively easy task to toss them back upon the foe, who, dressed in light and loose attire, suffered far more than the chevaliers cased in steel.

Exhaustion, however, was now the prevailing condition on both sides. While the few but heroic defenders were losing strength under the daily exertions which they had to maintain against climate as well as their foes, the Turks began also to suffer from disease, and lost quite 800 men by dysentery. Viperan complacently talks of poison placed in the wells by the garrison.

The Viceroy of Sicily, Garcia del Toledo, now sent over a confidential agent, Salazar, to make a personal inspection of the state of things in the island. Salazar made his way to Citta Vecchia, from whence, with the escort of 100 horse, he reached, in the early hours of 22nd August, the

MALTA AND THE GREAT SIEGE 79

village of Tarschien. From thence, with five companions, he walked towards the Turkish camp, where he found the sentinels asleep; so passing on to the extremity of the works, he observed that there were only twelve paces between the advanced posts of the besiegers and the walls of the Borgo. He then retired undiscovered.

Salazar returned to Sicily on the 23rd August, and on the 25th the relieving force set sail from Syracuse, where 145 ships had been collected by Garcia.

They did not, however, start with the unanimous approval of Garcia's council of war, one of whom absolutely stated that he thought the best termination of the campaign would be that the Turks should exterminate the knights, and be themselves exterminated by the Spanish force. Such may have been Philip's opinion, but when the Protestant Queen of England had ordered public prayers in the churches for the defenders of Christendom, the Catholic King could hardly hold back.

Unfortunately stormy weather ensued during the next few days, and the fleet had to put back more than once. That this storm was no fiction we learn from other sources, as an attack projected by the Turks was rendered ineffective, they declared, by the weather, which rendered their artillery unserviceable. It was in the interval of one of these tempestuous days that the garrison contrived to destroy by fire a large moveable tower which the Turks had raised. At last the assailants' columns had to be driven up to the charge by blows from the flat of their officers' sabres, while the defenders simply cut down those who headed the charge, and the rest gave way. When the Grand Master could send a messenger to Notabile, and he could return unmolested, the last stage had been almost reached.

The rapidity with which the evacuation took place shows the state of discomfiture to which the besiegers had been reduced. On the morning of the 7th September, 8,500 men landed from Sicily at Melleha Bay, and the fleet returned for 4,000 more, and supplies. During that night the enemy removed their war material to their ships, and on the next morning all their posts were abandoned.[1] The garrison at once re-occupied St. Elmo, and harassed the retreating Turks. When, however, Mustapha learned the extent of the succour afforded, he landed at St. Paul's Bay 9,000 men, intending to march up to the old capital. On their road thither they began an irregular skirmish with the vanguard of the relieving army, which had been posted near Musta by the commander-in-chief, Ascaneo Corneo.

Alvarez Sandeo, commanding the detachment,

---

[1] Pictures of the main incidents in the war were painted in 1601 by Matteo d'Aleccio to adorn the walls of the palace, which, thirty years later, were engraved at Bologna.

MALTA AND THE GREAT SIEGE 81

could not restrain their impetuosity, and, as the Turks gave way, a general flight and pursuit took place. This was checked at the point of embarkation by the rearguard under Hassan, but the Moslems were fain to re-embark after considerable loss, and made the best of their way to Constantinople, their numbers having been reduced to 15,000 at most. The gallant garrison had likewise suffered severely, barely 600 being left without some wound to tell of their victory.

A recent French writer (1887) puts the loss of life at 260 knights and nearly 8,000 soldiers in the defending force, and estimates that of the Turks at 30,000 men.

No wonder that all Christendom joined in contributing to the erection on Mount Schebarras of a town to bear the name of the hero who had commanded in such a splendid campaign of endurance and bravery.

CHAPTER VI

THE GRAND MASTERS OF MALTA

THE glorious issue of the struggle for Malta confirmed the Order of St. John in the position of a sovereign independent community. The Grand Master surmounted his escutcheon with a crown, received ambassadors, and sent envoys to foreign courts. Of the magnificence with which successive rulers of the Order kept their state, the city of palaces, Valletta, with its wealth of art treasures bears testimony, though shorn by French rapacity of much of its splendour. Public buildings, provided by the bounty of individual knights, aqueducts, gardens, causeways, and a hundred other improvements converted the formerly barren island rock into a land of milk and honey, and the inhabitants reaped the fruit of an expenditure maintained by the tribute of all Europe from Lisbon to Warsaw, wherever a commandery of the Order was seated.

Nor were the knights forgetful of their obligations as defenders of Christendom. Not content with repelling the attacks upon their island shores, their fleet went out for an annual cruise and brought back the spoil of the captured Asiatic or African corsairs, and the Christian slaves who were chained to the oar of the Moslem galley saw their tyrants compelled to change places with them. The knights were not always successful, it is true, but the part which these cruises played in the gradual extinction of piracy has scarcely been sufficiently taken into consideration by the historian of the sixteenth and two following centuries.

In these transactions, however, England had no share. The events which succeeded the Reformation completely scattered the British Langue. Some of its members suffered under the politico-religious severities of the Tudor dynasty, others conformed, but few resorted to Malta. Oliver Starkey, secretary to Grand Master John de Vallette, is the only Englishman buried in St. John's.

There exists in the archives at Malta a very curious volume, recording the crimes committed by certain knights of the Order and the sentences passed upon them, during one hundred years after their establishment in the island. The compiler of this black list notes that different nations were disposed to commit offences of different kinds, and especially with regard to England that turbulence and insubordination were their leading faults. For instance, in 1535 three English cavaliers (*milites venerandæ linguæ Anglicanæ*), Christopher Myres, David Guyon, and Philip Babington, fought "even to the effusion of blood," with their fists apparently, and were punished by solitary confinement and bread and water.

More serious, however, was the case of the Turcopolier Clement West, who, having been appointed to that office by L'Isle Adam, Grand Master, in 1531, was deprived of the habit and dignity for insubordinate conduct in 1533, and after being restored to his rank in 1535 was again deprived and imprisoned in 1539. What were the exact motives to this transaction we are unaware. West died in 1547.

The Auberge d'Angleterre, a plain building of small dimensions, and latterly ruinous, stood at the upper end of the Strada Reale until, under English rule, its site was occupied by the Opera House. Successive Grand Masters held in trust the official post of Turcopolier, probably to avoid the possibility of its being appropriated to some other Langue. Twice overtures were made towards a resuscitation of the English Langue. Once in the later years of the seventeenth century, when James II. entertained a hope of reconciliation between Great Britain and the Vatican, a gallant soldier, the Duke of Berwick, who derived his parentage from the King, was admitted to the Order notwithstanding his illegitimacy, and hopes were entertained that many of the noble families who adhered to the "ancient faith," or to the royal House

THE GRAND MASTERS OF MALTA 85

of Stuart, might follow his example, but with no discernible result. Again, in the closing era of the sovereignty of the Grand Masters, De Rohan built an auberge for what he designated the revived Anglo-Bavarian Langue, with which he incorporated the Grand Priory of Poland; but although Bavarians and Poles became members of the new Langue, its connection with England was nominal only.

It is somewhat singular that the last actual admixture of Englishmen with the transactions of the Order in Malta can hardly be called creditable to either side. General Porter says that during the earlier portion of the sway of the Grand Masters they bore their part manfully in the naval contests which were so frequently carried on with the Turkish maritime power. As, however, that empire gradually became less and less formidable, so did the martial energy of the fraternity steadily diminish. Their naval superiority so far dwindled that their fleet became a mere appanage intended for show, and not very available for service. The so-called caravans of the galleys were mere pleasure cruises to the various ports of the south of Europe. Toronini, in his "Travels in Egypt," gives the following description of the Maltese galleys at this period: "They were armed, or rather embarrassed, with an incredible number of hands; the 'General' alone, the flagship of the Order, had eight hundred men on board. They were superbly ornamented: gold blazed on the numerous *basso relievos* and sculptures on the stern; enormous sails, striped blue and white, carried on their centre a great cross of Malta painted red; their elegant flags floated majestically: in a word, everything concurred when they were under sail to render it a magnificent spectacle; but their construction was little adapted either for fighting or for standing foul weather. The Order kept them up rather as an image of its ancient splendour than for their utility. It was one of those ancient institutions which had once served to render the brotherhood illustrious, but now only attested its selfishness and decay."

The Admiralty in its decrepitude endeavoured to supplement its fighting deficiences by the grant of letters of marque to adventurers of all races, notably English, whose unscrupulous exploits caused (as Marryat has told us) the term Malta privateer to be equivalent to pirate. Prominent among these rovers in the middle of the eighteenth century was Ferdinand Wright, whose name deserved to be bracketed with those of Cochrane and Paul Jones. He succeeded so well on his expeditions that, as we learn from Lord Charlemont, who was residing in Malta in 1756 or 1757, the French actually fitted up another privateer of superior force to attack him. An action took place in the Malta channel; the ramparts of Valletta were crowded with partisans of France; two ships appeared in sight with French colours flying, but in the midst of the jubilation the white flag suddenly gave place to the English colours: the French vessel was a prize to the English ship.

It ought, however, to be observed that the last fleet of the Order which left Valletta was charged with material for the relief of the sufferers by the earthquake in Sicily in 1783. The spirit of the old hospitallers was maintained to the end.

It must not be forgotten that the composition of the Order contained in itself elements of disturbance. Its members were, for the most part, arrogant young men of rank, whom desire of adventure, or impatience of the restraints of home, had brought into the ranks of the knights, for in those days there were no rival safety valves in the attractions of colonial life or adventurous sport. So long as active warfare could be found for such spirits they were the best and bravest support of the Christian cause, but in the peaceful routine of the intervals between the expeditions against the corsairs they would chafe at discipline and perhaps defy authority from mere *ennui*. In some cases peccadilloes large or small had been the secret spring of their admission to the Convent, and, judging from the list to which I have already referred, the number of expulsions from the Order (*priva del' abito*) indicates that the black sheep were not a few.

The reports of visitors to Malta such as Dryden and Sandys confirm this view; but more favourable evidence as to the state of the society of the Auberges in the seventeenth century is to be found in

88 HOSPITALLERS OF ST. JOHN

the adventures of Count George Albert of Erbach,[1] translated from the German by a Royal Lady of Justice in our own Order. As a picture of the life of Malta in the most flourishing period of the supremacy of the Grand Masters it is unsurpassed, full of variety and yet faithful in delineation.

The hospital work primarily attracts our attention. The knights on their arrival found a hospital already existing in the ancient capital of the island; as, however, their purpose was to remove the seat of government to the Castle of St. Angelo on the northern side of the island, it was in the Borgo, the town at the rear of the fort, that their own first hospital was founded, whose gateway, of some architectural merit, still exists in the buildings of a more modern nunnery. In 1575, some forty years later, a larger hospital was erected in the new city of Valletta, on the south-east side of the promontory and close to the entrance to the great harbour, a less airy situation than the other extremity of the town would have been, but with this advantage, that it had a passage communicating with the sea front, through which sick or wounded patients might be landed from shipboard without being carried up and down the declivities of the steep streets of the rocky town. This building still exists, and is in

---

[1] "Count Albert of Erbach, a true story translated from the German by Beatrice, Princess Henry of Battenberg." London: John Murray, 1891.

THE GREAT HOSPITAL AT MALTA.
From an old print, 1630.

use as one of our military hospitals. In size and importance it is worthy of the traditions of its founders, although the Report of the Barrack and Hospital Commission of 1863 sweepingly condemned it for want of ventilation, of window space, and for its situation near a sewer. These defects, however, have been to a great extent satisfactorily dealt with; new windows have been opened, balconies facing the sea erected, and solid cement has replaced the friable stone of the original floor. The sewerage is now entirely diverted from the vicinity. The great ward, 503 feet long, is a magnificent interior, though necessarily divided by partitions of 15 feet high, the height of the apartment itself being 30 ft. 6 in. In the early days of its foundation the arrangements and service were on a most costly and elaborate scale. Utensils of silver, hangings and pictures, canopies to the beds whence depended mosquito curtains, and a "fortnightly" supply of clean linen, excited the admiration of the English travellers Sandys and Teonge.

The hospital, called the Infermeria (to quote from the "Adventures of Count George Albert of Erbach"), was situated in a large new building, and presided over by the Regent of the French Knights, the Great Hospitaller, who had under him five doctors, graduated in the medical college, and three apothecaries. The tending of the sick was carried out by knights and servants from time to time deputed for this service.[1] Sick and wounded knights, their servants standing at their bedsides, were lying in a large luxurious apartment, carpeted with oriental stuffs. One hundred and fifty beds were constantly held ready for knights who might return from the expeditions sick or wounded. Every bed had its special covering, on which was worked the cross of the Order, and at the head was a board, on which the doctor's directions for the patient's food were inscribed. At the end of the long apartment stood a small altar, at which Mass was daily said. In a second room were the beds for the servants and slaves; and such as suffered from repulsive or incurable complaints were nursed in inner wards quite apart. All these rooms were on the ground floor, over which were others with windows tightly closed; to these wards were brought those knights whose wounds affected vital organs, for in such cases it had been proved by experience that the fine, penetrating sea air was most pernicious.

Howard[2] at the end of the eighteenth century

---

[1] The regulations of 1725 prescribe a daily routine of attendance.
    La Domenica per la lingua di Provenza.
    Il Lunedi per quella di Alvernia.
    Il Martedi per quella di Francia.
    Il Mercoldi per quella d'Italia.
    Il Giovedi per quella d'Aragona.
    Il Venerdi per quella d'Alemagna.
    Il Sabato per Castiglia e Portugallo.
[2] " Lazarettos in Europe," 1789, p. 58.

THE GRAND MASTERS OF MALTA 91

(1789) speaks very strongly of the shameful negligence and incompetence of the management of the hospital at that time, but the book of Regulations of 1725[1] (reprinted in 1882) shows that this slackness was not normal, but attributable to causes affecting the well-being of the Order generally. As General Porter has reminded us, these faults were due to that "state of decline when it only required a bold hand or a national convulsion to sweep the knights away from the scene altogether." The Hospital was placed in the particular charge of the French Langue. At the time of the death of the Grand Master de Rohan, nearly three-fifths of the knights resident at headquarters were members of one or other of the three French Langues, whom contemporary testimony describes as discontented, needy, and extravagant. Many of them had imbibed the infidel and levelling ideas of the philosophic school at that date supreme among their countrymen at home, and all viewed with anxiety the rising cloud of political change which was becoming visible.

It is noticeable in the list of Grand Hospitallers of the eighteenth century, that two years was the limit for which, as a rule, each occupied the post, though occasionally a second term was added, and more rarely a third. The number of servants had been by that time reduced, and the pewter dishes

[1] "Regulations of the Hospital of St. John" (Blackwood, 1882).

originally confined to the *gente di catena*, or criminal patients, had found their way into the upper ward, where the ordinary subjects of charity were treated. The fact that the use of perfumes was habitual in the hospital is rightly commented on by Howard as a proof of inattention to cleanliness and airiness, a charge which he brings home by his own personal observation.

In 1796 (little more than a year before the final demolition of the sovereignty of the Order) new regulations were promulgated for the Hospital, from which we learn that the number of patients was computed at from 350 to 400, for whom 38 attendants were to be provided. The summary of the annual accounts from May 1, 1795, to April 30, 1796, gives an expenditure for food—viz., baked bread, wine, oil, flour, raisins, meat, and vermicelli—of 48,866 scudi.

Howard mentions a foundling hospital, where he saw a number of fine healthy children, and thirty-nine girls from seven to about twelve years of age; also a hospital for women with 230 beds, described as offensive and dirty, and two houses for the poor, containing 140 males and 213 females, of whose condition he speaks favourably. It is in connection with this last house that the curious piece of misapplied ingenuity, which still excites the wonder of sightseers, "the chapel of bones," was originally constructed.

The disastrous part of the story of the Malta hos-

THE GRAND MASTERS OF MALTA 93

pital is the bargain which, under French influence, the members of the Order were induced to make with the Antonines. It was this. In 1095 the nobles of Dauphigny founded a fraternity of Hospitallers (erected into the regular Antonine Order in 1218) for the relief of sufferers under St. Anthony's fire. In 1777 an arrangement was made that the Order of St. John should take over the property of this Antonine fraternity, subject to various conditions which involved an excess of expenditure which in ten years (1787) had reached 732,947 scudi; but it was calculated that in 1794 the income would return, and go on increasing until 1879, when the outlay with interest would be recovered by the treasury, and the annual income reach 120,000 French livres. The Antonine estates were situated in France and Savoy. In 1792 the property of the Order in France was confiscated. Thus not only the three Langues of France, Auvergne, and Provence lost the income from their commanderies, but the Order lost its revenue from responsions and other dues of the estates, a sum estimated at 471,784 scudi, exclusive of the Antonine estates, upon which the Order up to 1792 must have lost a million scudi.[1]

This loss, coming upon an already depleted income, must have dealt the final blow to the solvency of the Valletta treasury. The malcontents from this time had the upper hand in the affairs of the Order.

[1] Scudo equivalent to a dollar.

On the death of Grand Master de Rohan, in 1796, Ferdinand von Hompesch, a Knight of the German Langue, was elected his successor, a man who neither possessed the ability nor the influence necessary to cope with the treachery with which he was encompassed. In 1798 Napoleon Bonaparte, on his expedition to Egypt, landed part of his army, and after three days' negotiation Valletta was surrendered into his hands, for, as an English historian puts it, " The capitulation of the place had been previously secured by secret intelligence with the Grand Master and principal officers." This at least is certain, that a powerful party being ready to support the pretensions of the French, the government was a prey to dissension at a moment when unanimity was the only chance of safety. Preparations for defence had been altogether neglected, and in the midst of panic and confusion the terms of capitulation were hastily slurred over. To the Grand Master was promised a principality in Germany or a pension for life of 300,000 francs ; the French knights were to receive a pension of 700 francs apiece ; and a promise was given that the property of the inhabitants should not be confiscated, nor their religion disturbed. Thus, says Bartlett, "ignominiously came to a close, on June 12, 1798, the once illustrious Order of St. John of Jerusalem, having subsisted for more than 700 years. At this time its members consisted of 200 French knights,

THE GRAND MASTERS OF MALTA 95

90 Italian, 25 Spanish, 8 Portuguese, and 5 Anglo-Bavarian—in all 328, of whom 50 were disabled by age and infirmities. The military force amounted to 7,100 men, which might easily have been increased to 10,000."

The French might well congratulate themselves upon the ease with which they gained possession of such a stronghold. It is said that Napoleon, walking round the bastions, suddenly stopped and exclaimed, "What sublime fortifications!" to which his chief of the staff, Caffarelli, replied, " It is well, general, that there was some one within to open the gates to us. We should have had more trouble in working our way through had the place been empty." The works were at once put into an effective state for defence, and the bastions furnished with 1,000 cannon. Leaving General Vaubois with a garrison of 3,000 men, and carrying off with him all the disciplined soldiery as well as the liberated Turkish galley slaves, Bonaparte set sail for Egypt on the 19th June, after rifling St. John's of its treasures, and seizing every scrap of valuable bullion or art work which could be gleaned from the public edifices or the churches.

The indignation of the Maltese people was excessive at finding themselves thus betrayed. With great difficulty they were persuaded not to attempt to hold the principal forts in Valletta on their own account, and several of the treacherous knights were put to death in a tumult which arose at the surrender. The news of Nelson's victory at Aboukir emboldened them to rise in open insurrection against their oppressors. A body of soldiers were about to despoil the cathedral at Citta Vecchia, when the populace overpowered and dispersed them; and the whole island arming against the French, the latter had to shut themselves up within the walls of Valletta, where they were hemmed in by the insurgents and blockaded by an English fleet, which landed some regular troops, as well as arms and ammunition for the natives, and vigorously invested them by sea and land for a period of two years. After enduring the extremity of famine and disease, which indeed seriously affected the besieging force also, and carried off thousands of Maltese, the brave French commandant, with only a few quarters of wheat left in his stores, surrendered to General Pigot, commanding the English forces.

Besides co-operating with ships and soldiers in the deliverance of Malta from its invaders, the English, with the entire consent of the natives, who had elected Nelson's representative, Captain Sir Alexander Ball, as their governor, assumed the civil direction of its affairs. At the Peace of Amiens an attempt was made to reconstitute the Order as ruling authority in the island, under the protection of the Great Powers of Europe; but the Maltese people themselves most strenuously protested against this,

THE GRAND MASTERS OF MALTA 97

and Bonaparte, who is reported to have said that he would as soon endure to see the English in possession of a faubourg of Paris as of a fortress of Malta, did in fact renew the war on this account. On the 15th of June, 1802, the members of a congress elected by the free suffrages of the Maltese people solemnly made over the sovereignty of the island to the King of Great Britain and his successors. At the Congress of Vienna, 1814, the conflicting claims were settled in favour of the British Government, the possession of the island finally confirmed to them, and the following inscription placed on the Main Guard, in the square of St. George, opposite the palace:

MAGNAE ET INVICTAE BRITANNIAE
MELITENSIUM AMOR
ET
EUROPAE VOX
HAS INSULAS CONFIRMAT [1]
A.D. 1814.

[1] The inscription runs thus, "confirmat," in the original.

CHAPTER VII

THE ENGLISH REVIVAL

WHILE Malta, thanks to the patriotism of its native population and the generous disinterestedness of their English allies, was shaking off the yoke of the French invaders, those who so basely invited the aggression of the enemy were experiencing the disappointment which their treachery merited. Instead of the promised possessions and pecuniary bribes which had been dangled before them, the craven knights received only 250 francs [1] apiece by way of indemnity, and were ignominiously expelled from their island. They dispersed in various directions. A few took service with the French army, and less than a score accompanied the fallen Grand Master to Trieste, whence some of them found their way to St. Petersburg.

Some kind of friendly negotiation had been in progress with the autocrat of Russia as long before this as 1782, when Grand Master de Rohan projected the foundation of his Anglo-Bavarian Langue. He sought at that time the sanction of the English monarch to the use of the title of the Sixth Langue,

[1] "Edin. Review," 1901.

AUBERGE DE BAVIERE, MALTA, SHOWING THE SPIRE OF QUEEN ADELAIDE'S CHURCH.

THE ENGLISH REVIVAL 99

and as he also proposed to unite with it the Grand Priory of Poland, he entered into correspondence with the Empress Catherine II. as to that portion of her subjects who adhered to the Greek Church. This led to a large migration of refugee knights to St. Petersburg, where Paul was now on the throne, and they were cordially welcomed by the Czar. With the tacit assent of the Grand Master this fragmentary section of the Order assembled in conclave at St. Petersburg on October 27th, 1798, and elected the Czar as Grand Master of the Order, though no formal resignation by Hompesch had yet taken place. Paul accepted the election on November 13th of the same year, and on the 10th December was privately invested. He appears, however, to have insisted upon a formal resignation by Hompesch, who shortly afterwards retired to Montpellier, where he joined one of the strictest fraternities of penitents, and died in complete obscurity in 1805.

Although Hompesch did not himself repair to St. Petersburg, he caused two of the most valued relics of the Order which he had brought from Malta to be presented to the Emperor Paul. One was the hand of St. John, the gift of Sultan Bajazet to Grand Master d'Aubusson, which had been kept in a gauntlet-shaped case of solid gold, richly bejewelled, in the church of St. John. It is said that Bonaparte took the great sapphire ring which lay in front of the case (the offering of a monarch in the fifteenth century) and put it on his own finger, desiring the case itself to be taken on board the flagship, and contemptuously adding, "You may keep the carrion."

The other great relic now at St. Petersburg is the icon of Our Lady of Philermos, cherished by the Order at Rhodes as a kind of Palladium, and now in the chapel of the Imperial Winter Palace at St. Petersburg.[1] This too was one of the treasures of St. John's, and from its chapel the French took bullion of the value of £1,200.

The historian Sutherland thus refers to this election of the Russian Czar: "An election which placed a prince, bound by matrimonial ties and beyond the pale of the Catholic Church, at the head of the Order, shattered at once the very basis on which it was founded: indeed as the act of a few refugee knights, who in their despair grasped at a reed in the hope that it would support them, some writers argue that it ought to form no part or parcel of the legal proceedings of the Order. Be this as it may, the election was bitterly reprobated by the Pope; and the Elector of Bavaria, to get rid of the disputes in which it involved him, abolished the Order in his dominions."

About this period English influence seems to have been paramount in the disposal of the honours of

[1] See a privately printed pamphlet by the late Sir George Bowyer, in the Library at St. John's Gate.

THE ENGLISH REVIVAL

St. John. One of the first appointments made by Paul was the bestowal of the decoration of *Dame Chevalière* upon Emma, Lady Hamilton, and in the correspondence of Napoleon occurs the following: "Give orders to have Kuhn, American Consul at Genoa, put under arrest for wearing a Cross of Malta given him by the English. His papers will be seized . . . and he will be kept in strict confinement until you have made your report to me."[1]

Before he ceased to be Grand Master it is certain that Hompesch invited the accession to the Order of certain English gentlemen of rank and distinction, several of whom survived to join the restored Order in England. Among these were Sir Sydney Smith, Sir W. Johnstone Hope (Governor of Greenwich Hospital), Sir Home Popham, Sir Richard Laurence, and Sir Joshua Colles Meredith, who conferred upon the late Sir Edward Perrott the accolade which he had himself received from the Grand Master.

Upon the death of the Emperor Paul in 1801, the Emperor Alexander assumed the title of Protector of the Order, and by decree dated the 16th March of that year appointed as his lieutenant Count Nicholas de Soltikoff, to exercise the functions and authority of the Grand Master. A council of Russian knights, calling themselves "The Sovereign Council of the Order," was assembled on the 20th June, 1801,

[1] "Letters of Napoleon I.," Lady Mary Loyd.

when it was decreed that the provincial chapters should select fitting candidates from amongst the professed knights of every language, and that his Holiness Pope Pius VII. should be entreated to select a Grand Master from these candidates.

It may be well supposed that, in its dismembered and desolate condition at this period, no deliberate or united action could be exercised by the scattered branches of the Order; probably some kind of presentation was made to the Pope, as the Bailiff de Ruspoli, a member of the Italian Langue, and formerly General of the galleys, was nominated by his Holiness; that knight, however, having declined on the plea of ill-health, two other dignitaries were successively selected, but they never entered upon the exercise of the office. At length, upon the recommendation of the Emperor Alexander and the King of Naples, his Holiness appointed the Count Giovanni di Tommasi on the 9th February, 1802. Tommasi proclaimed his appointment in the Priory Church, Messina, on the 27th June, 1802, and retained the dignity of Grand Master until his death in June, 1805. Before that event he had nominated the Bailiff Guévara Suardo to succeed him as Lieutenant of the Mastery, and this nomination was confirmed by the Pope.

No active attempt has been made to elect a Grand Master since the death of Tommasi, and the Lieutenant of the Mastery, Guévara Suardo, was suc-

THE ENGLISH REVIVAL 103

ceeded in that office by Giovanni y Centellès (1814), Count Antoine Busca (1812), Prince de Candida (1834), Count Colloredo (1845), Count Alexander Borgia (1865), and the Chevalier Cherchi de Santa Torre (1872). The residence of these officials was transferred from Catania to Ferrara in 1826, whence it was removed to Rome in 1834, where it still remains.

"It may be desirable at this point," says Porter, "to refer to Sir Bernard Burke's account of the foreign branches of the Order, as enumerated in his ' Book of Orders of Knighthood.' It is there stated that in Austria, the Papal States, Prussia, Russia and Spain, the Order of St. John existed in 1858. In Prussia the Bailiwick of Brandenburg separated itself from the Order in 1319, and assumed an independent existence; but after much disputation an agreement was made on the 11th June, 1382, between the Prior of Germany and the Bailiff of Brandenburg, by which the Knights of the Bailiwick should have at all times authority and power to elect their Bailiff. This agreement was not, however, confirmed for some years; subsequently the Bailiwick became in part allied with the general Order, notwithstanding its change to a Protestant form of religion. Ultimately in 1810 the estates of the Bailiwick were by royal edict incorporated with those of the Crown, and on the 23rd May, 1812, Frederick William III. remodelled this branch under the title of 'The Royal Prussian Order of St. John.' Referring to the Russian Priories, Sir Bernard says: 'The two Russian Grand Priorates still preserve the appearance of the old constitutions and form, under the protection and patronage of the Emperor, who is head of the Chapter; its connection with the Chapter at Rome is of a very loose character.' Such is the present state of the foreign branches of the Order."

It now remains to narrate the circumstances which attended the revival of the English Langue, as summarized in 1880.[1]

"The fall of Napoleon and the restoration of the Bourbons in 1814 removed the ban under which the French knights had lain since the edict of the 19th September, 1792. They at once reassembled in a Chapter-General at Paris, and, forming as they did at that time the most powerful branch of the Order still surviving, elected a Permanent Capitular Commission, in which was vested plenary power to act as might seem best for the general interests of the fraternity. The formation of this Capitular Commission was confirmed by a Pontifical Bull issued by Pope Pius VII. on the 10th August, 1814, and recognized by the Lieutenant of the Mastery and Sacred Council in an instrument dated the 9th October following, addressed to the Bailli Camille

[1] "The English or Sixth Langue," compiled by a Committee, 1880.

THE ENGLISH REVIVAL 105

Prince de Rohan, Prior of Aquitaine; the Bailli de Clugny; the Commander de Bataille (representing the Langue of France); the Commander de Peyre de Chateauneuf (representing the Langue of Provence); the Commander de Dienne (representing the Langue of Auvergne); the Commander Bertrand; and the Bailli Lasterie du Saillent, Prior of Auvergne. It also received the recognition of the King, Louis XVIII.

"This commission exercised important acts on behalf of the Order in general during a series of years; it negotiated, though unsuccessfully, with the King for the restoration of the property of the Order in France; it treated in 1814 with the Congress of Vienna for a new Chef Lieu in the Mediterranean. In an appeal to the French King and Chambers it represented the whole Order in 1816, and again at the Congress of Verona in 1822. Also as recorded by Sutherland: 'In 1823, when the Greek cause began to wear a prosperous aspect, the same Chapter, encouraged by the goodwill which the Bourbon family was understood to entertain for the Order, entered into a treaty with the Greeks for the cession of Sapienza and Cabressa, two islets on the western shore of the Morea, as a preliminary step to the reconquest of Rhodes, to facilitate which arrangement an endeavour was made to raise a loan of £40,000 in England.'

"Whilst engaged in these various negotiations

for the benefit of the Order at large, the question was mooted of a possible revival of the English Langue, which question speedily received a practical solution. The Commission placed themselves in communication with the Rev. Sir Robert Peat, D.D., Chaplain Extraordinary to his Majesty George IV., and other English gentlemen of position, to whom were submitted the documents constituting the commission. These gentlemen undertook to give their aid in the resuscitation of so interesting a relic of the ancient chivalry of Europe. The negotiations, which were continued for some months, resulted in the revival of the English Langue of the Order of St. John of Jerusalem, for which purpose Articles of Convention were executed on the 11th June, 1826,[1] and on the 24th August and 15th October, 1827. These documents thus refer to the English people:

"'This brave and generous nation furnished formerly illustrious subjects, who made part of the most formidable, the most valiant, and the most renowned Chevaliers of this ancient Sovereign Order, and whose successors are now invited to raise that Christian and famous banner which was in former times the pride and glory of their ancestors, and who can again form part of this Order in climates and in countries the most fortunate and most celebrated.'

[1] See "Notes and Queries," 1863, etc.

THE ENGLISH REVIVAL 107

"The articles of convention distinctly recite that in making this revival the French Langues are acting with the concurrence and approval of those of Arragon and Castile, thus, by a representation of five out of the eight divisions of the Order, giving the weight of majority, if such addition were necessary to the powers of the associated French Langues. That the revival of the Order in England was conducted and accomplished in the most honourable spirit and with the most chivalric intentions is indisputable. The English gentlemen whose interest was enlisted in the revival were men of the highest character, distinguished by superior attainments, to whose motives no suspicion can attach, whilst the disinterested views of the French Chevaliers may be gathered from a passage in one of their official communications, in which they declare that the business of the Order in England must be conducted in an English manner, and so that the foreign members should not interfere in the management of the funds, which were to be solely and exclusively under the direction of the English brethren. These communications, further enjoin the greatest caution in the nomination of Chevaliers, and declare that 'to revive so honourable an institution it is most necessary to act legally and according to the existing statutes, otherwise the Order would not be esteemed and respected, that the statutes must be taken by the Committee as its guide and direction in the work, and that from this foundation no departure could take place, except as regards the modifications necessary owing to the religion of the United Kingdom.'

"The Chevalier Philippe de Chastelain and Mr. Donald Currie were appointed delegates for formally inaugurating the revival, by deed dated December 14th, 1827.

"On the 24th of January, 1831, the Chevalier de Chastelain attended a meeting in London, when the English Langue was formally reorganized, and the Rev. Sir Robert Peat, D.D., Knight Grand Cross of the Royal Order of St. Stanislaus of Poland, and Chaplain Extraordinary to George IV., was invested with the functions and authority of Grand Prior of the revived English Langue. The names of many English noblemen and gentlemen were inscribed on the roll of the Langue, and its proceedings were conducted in full assurance of its perfect and lawful revival.[1]

"From that time the Langue has continued to advance in numbers and prosperity. Much opposition has been offered to it by those who have disputed the legitimacy of its revival, but their efforts to arrest its progress have been unavailing. Negotiations continued to be carried on for many years with the Roman branch with a view to secure an alliance, at first with every hope of success. The

[1] See Appendix IV.

THE ENGLISH REVIVAL 109

bona fides of the acts under which the Langue was revived never underwent the shadow of suspicion until the year 1858. The only difficulty brought forward before that date was the question of religion, a difficulty which had in former years been overcome in the case of the Protestant Knights of Brandenburg."

So far the chronicle. But when its compiler wrote these pages in 1880 he little foresaw that a decade would not elapse ere the English Order would obtain the highest authoritative sanction possible, in the shape of a Charter from her Most Gracious Majesty Queen Victoria. We may briefly glance at the reasons for this favourable change in the prospects of the English branch. Of course when first revived its position was but precarious, and among its adherents might be some who sought no other ends than those of which Mr. Kemble speaks with well-deserved scorn in his preface to the volume already quoted, "The Hospitallers in England." But the spirit which actuated the majority of its members was widely at variance with mere idle ostentation. Sir Edward Perrott was long and honourably connected with the Life-boat movement. Mr. (now Sir John) Furley and Sir V. Kennett Barrington were both active in ambulance work in war between the years 1870 and 1880; but it was not until the rise and amazing progress of the Ambulance Department of the Order in instruction in the first treatment of injured persons, that it obtained the national recognition which it now enjoys, justifying on that ground alone the refoundation of the Order in England. Among those who conduced most essentially to this end, two names ought to be recorded, the more so because, alas, they are both gone from us:

> Only the actions of the just
> Smell sweet and blossom in the dust.

Sir Edmund Lechmere became a member of the Order in December, 1865, and was appointed its Secretary in 1867. He was among the first to join the National Society for aid to the sick and wounded in war in 1870. He had already established a commandery of the Order at Hanley Castle, which did good service in Worcestershire in assisting the hospitals there by providing nourishing food for discharged patients. In 1874 he was instrumental in the acquisition of St. John's Gate by the Order. From the commencement of the Ambulance Department he was prominent in his support of it, and he originated and strenuously supported the Ophthalmic Hospital at Jerusalem, of which he was Chairman in 1894, the year of his death.

Colonel Francis Duncan, a soldier, a politician, and a man of rare eloquence, joined the Ambulance Department as Director in 1875, and for the next ten years was the life and soul of the movement

KNIGHT OF JUSTICE.   KNIGHT OF GRACE.

The embellishment for a Knight of Justice is in gold, and for a Knight of Grace in silver.

THE ENGLISH REVIVAL

which has taken so great a hold of the people of England.

The Charter was granted in 1888, and in the same year the installation of H.R.H. the Prince of Wales as Grand Prior, in succession to the Duke of Manchester, took place. H.R.H. the Duke of Clarence and Avondale was appointed Sub-Prior, an office which, on the lamented death of the Prince, was conferred upon H.R.H. the Duke of York, who has succeeded his royal father as Grand Prior upon his Majesty's becoming the supreme Head and Patron of the Order of the Hospital in England of St. John of Jerusalem.

HAT AND SWORD OF LA VALLETTE.

CHAPTER VIII

THE AMBULANCE MOVEMENT

THE members of the revived English Order were some time in discovering the most practical mode in which they might carry into action the latter clause of their profession, *pro utilitate hominum*. It was indeed only by degrees that the great popular feature of their present work evolved itself. Its genesis is connected with the Red Cross movement, which was so actively progressive during the sixties. The Order of St. John of Jerusalem in England, as it then existed, was represented at the International Conference of Red Cross Societies held in Berlin in 1869; and when the Franco-German War broke out in the summer of 1870, many members of the Order enrolled themselves in the newly formed British National Aid (or Red Cross) Society, and were continuously engaged both at home and at the theatre of war throughout the campaign. At the conclusion of this war it became evident that no Red Cross Society could fulfil its duties in time of war unless its *personnel* and *matériel* were organized in time of peace. But it was not until February, 1878, that this opinion was definitely expressed at a

THE AMBULANCE MOVEMENT 113

public meeting held at the Pall Mall Restaurant under the presidency of Sir Edmund Lechmere. A guarantee fund was subscribed with a view to enabling the Order to enter without delay upon all necessary preparations in case of war. Major Duncan, as Director of the Ambulance Department, prepared a most careful and exhaustive report, which was approved and adopted by the Chapter.[1] Thus was commenced the great Ambulance movement which has met with such extensive support, and has benefited and educated the nation at large.

In March, 1878, it was unanimously decided that all ambulance work, whether carried on directly by the Order or indirectly through the St. John Ambulance Association, should be under the Ambulance Committee of the Order, a committee upon which none but members or associates could serve. This system has worked successfully : by means of it many members of the Order have been able to lend special help and supervision to hospitaller work in many parts of the country, and have felt a reality in their connection with an historical body, where hitherto, perhaps, there existed only sentiment and affection. It was also the means of attracting to the Order many new and distinguished members, who admired the modern and appropriate development

[1] "Origin and Development of the St. John Ambulance Association," Sir John Furley, 1897.

of so old and noble a work. And at the same
time the system provided a central administrative
and executive body, which could enforce rules and
make suggestions with an authority which no committee of men, unqualified by membership, could
claim. The many local committees scattered over
the Empire rendered a ready and loyal obedience to
this Central Committee. The growth of their work
continued to increase on a scale quite unprecedented.
Many public bodies, large towns, and important industrial centres had been reached by the exertions
of the central committees, and were availing themselves of that simple instruction in rendering aid to
the wounded which the Order of St. John was seek-
ing to place at the disposal of all. The list of such
centres of instruction was lengthened in the year
1878 by the addition of such towns as Portsmouth,
Southampton, Folkestone, Basingstoke, Ramsgate,
Nottingham, Halifax, Ferry Hill, Carlisle, White-
haven, Wrexham, Chester, Warrington, Bedford,
West Hartlepool, Stroud, and others. The city of
Dublin had been remarkably active and successful,
no fewer than thirty-five classes having been under
instruction containing no less than 1,213 pupils
during the year; and in addition to the centres,
detached classes under the direct supervision of
the Executive Committee were held at some fifty
new places, showing that the work was becoming
more generally understood and popular, and the

THE AMBULANCE MOVEMENT 115

employers of labour were beginning to realize its importance.

As far back as the year 1872 a sum of £100 had been given by a member of the Order "for the purpose of establishing an ambulance service, under the control of the Order, in the mining and pottery districts, where accidents are of frequent occurrence, and where there existed then no such organization."

This was soon followed by the purchase of two litters made in Berlin, which were similar in pattern to some used in the Prussian army. These were placed at Burslem and Wolverhampton respectively, private individuals and public bodies undertaking to defray expenses and to superintend the management. In a very short time quite a considerable business was done in German litters, and a large number were purchased for the use of the Metropolitan Police.

At the annual General Assembly of the Order held in 1874, a paper was read by Surgeon-General Thomas Laymon, C.B., entitled "Observations on the preliminary care and attention necessary for accidental bodily injuries and mutilations occurring in mines and establishments where many workpeople are employed." This was the first occasion at St. John's Gate on which broad lines were laid down by a competent authority on first aid to the injured.

On the following anniversary a paper was read on "The transport of sick and wounded by railway," by Surgeon Sandford Moore, Army Hospital Corps.

In July, 1876, a private meeting was held by a provisional committee of the Order of St. John, when it was resolved "That there being no organization in existence for giving relief, irrespective of political aim or object, a committee should be formed of members of the Order and others, for the purpose of affording such aid as possible to the sufferers in the conflict raging in the East." At this meeting the Eastern War Sick and Wounded Relief Fund was formed, which was subsequently merged in the British National Society for Aid to Sick and Wounded in War.

In June, 1877, a paper was read at the General Assembly of the Order on "The proper sphere of volunteer societies for the relief of sick and wounded soldiers in war," by Mr. (now Sir John) Furley.

A year later, at the same place, a lecture was given on "Some forms of extemporaneous conveyances for sick and wounded in peace and war," by Surgeon-Major J. H. Porter, Assistant Professor of Military Surgery at Netley.

In August, 1877, Mr. Furley had been requested by the Council of the British National Aid Society to proceed to Montenegro as Special Commissioner, with a view to his inquiring into the state of the hospitals and their requirements. He proceeded to

THE AMBULANCE MOVEMENT 117

Cettinge, and subsequently to Nichsics, in which fortress the Turks were at that time closely besieged. After having visited all the hospitals, suggested improvements in the system of transport for the sick and wounded, and relieved some pressing necessities, Mr. Furley returned to England, where he occupied himself in dispensing the sum placed at his disposal by the National Aid Society. His services were warmly acknowledged by Prince Nicholas and his ministers, as well as by the delegates in Montenegro of the Russian Red Cross Society.

Mr. V. Kennett Barrington, an Honorary Associate of the Order (now Sir Vincent Kennett Barrington), was selected by the Stafford House Committee as its commissioner, and, assisted by a very efficient staff, carried out the organization and direction of hospitals in no less than nine places in European Turkey and Asia, as well as field ambulances, a sanitary service, and the railway transport; and Dr. Laseron, an Honorary Associate, having superintended the nursing of the patients at the English hospital at Belgrade in 1876, organized a large hospital at Wardino, and afterwards proceeded to Rustchuck, where he opened a similar establishment, and received the gratitude of the recipients of his humane efforts.

During the Turco-Russian War the Viscountess Strangford went to the seat of war and commenced her good work among the sick and wounded amidst actual personal danger and many privations and difficulties. After the occupation by the Russians of Sophia at the close of the year 1877, all communication with the outer world being cut off, and unable to procure the supplies necessary for extending her work, Lady Strangford was in January, 1878, compelled to give up her hospital and send her nurses home to England. She proceeded herself to Constantinople, and removed thence to Scutari, where she re-established her hospital in two houses given her by the Sultan, and with untiring energy still occupied herself in tending the sick and wounded of the Order's ancient enemies. Nouri Pasha, the Surgeon-General of the Ottoman Army, inspected her hospital and pronounced it to be a model for others. Not far from the hospital Lady Strangford opened a home for children of the refugees, who were dying in great numbers from typhoid fever and starvation.

The St. John Ambulance Association was first mentioned in the Report for 1878 as a Department of the Order of St. John, but its management and finance were kept quite independent. The first centre was established at Woolwich, quickly followed by a Metropolitan centre, and the formation of centres at Sevenoaks, Maidstone, Worcester, Malvern, and Southampton. We may follow here Sir John Furley's careful and sympathetic narrative of progress:

THE AMBULANCE MOVEMENT 119

"In 1878 a great advance was made, especially amongst the Derbyshire and Nottingham collieries. The work was also taken up by the Metropolitan Police, and on one occasion at Scotland Yard, when there was a difficulty about the time for Police Classes, the men were asked by their officers whether they would prefer to forgo first-aid instruction or give up part of the dinner hour; all the policemen who were present replied that they would rather sacrifice the recreation time."

The course of instruction was usually limited to five lectures followed by an examination; and certificates were awarded to those who satisfied the examiner. But although the doctors generally extended the lectures beyond the prescribed number, it soon became apparent that a large proportion of the pupils were not content with first-aid lectures only, and therefore advanced classes were formed for women at St. Mary's Hospital, and for men at King's College and Westminster Hospitals. Subsequently these advanced classes, although not often held at hospitals, became general, and a second examination was held and a superior certificate was given.

It was in 1879 that the first manual of ambulance instruction ("Shepherd's Handbook") was published, and 26,000 copies were at once sold.[1]

[1] Up to 1897, 570,000 copies of "Shepherd's Handbook," and 110,000 copies of "Cosgrave's Manual," had been issued.

At this time also it was found necessary to establish a depot at St. John's Gate, from which all articles required for the lectures, such as handbooks, anatomical diagrams, bandages, splints, tourniquets, and stretchers, could be supplied.

Hitherto the Association had obtained its two-wheeled litters from Germany, and some of its stretchers from France; an ambulance wagon had also been purchased by special permission from the Royal Arsenal at Woolwich. Nor must the Esmarch triangular bandage, also made in Germany, be forgotten, as it was then, and still remains, the most popular article of an ambulancer's kit. But it was now felt that the time had arrived when improvements might be made, and a material adapted to the needs of the Association might be manufactured in England. A new stretcher was introduced, and this was soon followed by a two-wheeled litter of original design, which combined the stretcher with an undercarriage. Further progress was made when the Stores Department undertook the construction of horse-ambulance carriages.

Thus it will be seen that from a very humble commencement, namely, a two-wheeled litter and a triangular bandage from Germany, and a stretcher from France, a new industry had been established in England, and, instead of importing articles from the Continent, the Association was not only supplying the requirements of its numerous centres and

AMBULANCE WORKERS.

THE AMBULANCE MOVEMENT 121

detached classes throughout the United Kingdom, but it was also sending ambulance vehicles as models to foreign countries. A complete change was gradually being introduced. Previously, when an accident occurred, and it was necessary to carry an invalid in a recumbent position, a gate or a shutter had been considered to be the proper vehicle. This primitive method was, at any rate, very superior to the plan, still too frequently adopted, of doubling up a patient in a four-wheeled cab, regardless of the nature of his injuries.

The instruction of police all over the country soon became very general. In the Metropolitan Police classes were constantly at work, and the Secretary of State for the Home Department recognized the value of the instruction by an annual grant to cover the cost of handbooks and class material. A considerable improvement in the latter had been made by Mr. Furley. The excellent handbook of the late Surgeon-Major Shepherd had, after passing through a sale of thirty thousand copies, been revised by a medical sub-committee and republished in a similar form. Two handbooks for the nursing classes were also published. These classes for women were both popular and useful.

The ambulance wheeled litter, bearing the name and badge of the Order, was largely supplied to many of the most important provincial towns, and no less than thirty-eight were delivered to the Metropolitan Police in the year ending St. John's Day, 1881.

The recognition of the work among the police, which had been extended by the Home Secretary, enabled the Central Committee to carry out the methodical instruction of the Metropolitan Police in classes taught at Scotland Yard and other places, and the county and borough police generally throughout the country, and it was recognized that there was no class of men to whom this simple knowledge was more valuable, or by whom it could be more frequently put into practice. In the City and Port of London (through the generosity of the County Council and many of the City Companies) it was possible greatly to extend the instruction, also in the Royal Dockyards and at the Admiralty itself. A narrative of so gigantic a work as this would occupy too much space, but a light may be thrown on its dimensions by a few facts. In the six months commencing December, 1881, there was a total of 381 classes under instruction, and should an average of 40 pupils in each class be taken it will show a number of 15,240. This and many other successes may be explained by the fact that the want which the Order of St. John was meeting had been long felt, although it did not find methodical expression.

Except in the army a stretcher had been almost unknown outside a hospital, for we cannot recognize

THE AMBULANCE MOVEMENT 123

as such the rough and uncomfortable vehicle which was employed by the police and at union workhouses. The St. John Ambulance Association was not satisfied with simple improvements in its transport material, but by degrees it was educating the public to take an intelligent interest in the matter. If anyone inside the Association, or, in fact, outside of it, made suggestions with regard to alterations, a trial was immediately given, and if this proved satisfactory they were at once adopted; but those who were responsible for such changes declined to allow the name of the Association to be put to anything unless it was proved to be good. In this manner uniformity of material was obtained, one of the most important requirements in ambulance work either in peace or war. One single instance will be sufficient to exemplify the advantage of such uniformity. An invalid, in charge of a competent ambulancer, has been carried across Europe on one of the stretchers of the Association without having been once removed from it. The two-wheeled litter was used at the start, then the stretcher was conveyed by railway and steamboat, and one of the horse carriages from St. John's Gate completed the journey. This would have been impossible, had it not been known beforehand that the stretcher would fit the "Ashford" litter, or any one of the vehicles to be employed. This uniformity is a subject on which too great stress cannot be laid, more especially as the instruction given to the classes is, or should be, more or less, of a uniform character.[1]

In 1883 an effort was made to bring home first aid instruction to the officers and men of the mercantile marine, more particularly to those on vessels which go to sea without a doctor. The first attempts were made in the Port of London, and at Liverpool and Dover, and every encouragement was given by those officials at the Board of Trade whose position enabled them to exercise the greatest influence. It will be readily understood that, even with perfect goodwill on the part of the officers and men of the Merchant Service, there is no section of the community more difficult to reach. Every facility was afforded, and the lectures were compressed into the smallest possible time; but even then it was not easy to assemble classes at ports where men were engaged loading or unloading throughout each day, and naturally desired to go ashore and see their friends during the evening. The Board of Trade agreed to endorse the certificates of all officers who

---

[1] The extent of business done in the Stores Department since its establisment until the end of 1896 may be gathered from the following items: horse carriages issued, 64; litters, 952; stretchers, 3,943. And in 1898 the following were issued: 4 horse carriages, 50 Ashford litter under-carriages, 434 ambulance stretchers, and no less than 66,937 triangular and roller bandages. While in 1900, 8 ambulance carriages, 50 Ashford litter under-carriages, 641 ambulance stretchers, and 67,697 triangular and roller bandages were supplied.

THE AMBULANCE MOVEMENT 125

passed the ambulance examination, and to regard it as so much in a candidate's favour. This encouragement has acted as a considerable stimulus.

One great difficulty was soon recognized by the Central Committee. Hundreds of men and women of all grades of society were attending classes, passing examinations, and receiving certificates; but, as might be expected, a large proportion of these, from want of practice, speedily forgot what they had learned. It was therefore resolved, in July, 1879, that certificated pupils could be re-examined at the expiration of twelve months from the first examination; and subsequently it was settled that those who had twice undergone re-examination, in accordance with the terms of the resolution to which reference has just been made, with an interval of not less than twelve months between each examination, should be exempt from any further examination, and should be eligible to receive a medallion. Women who had passed the second-course examination—and this is what is called the nursing class, and especially adapted to women—were allowed to count this as re-examination, if the required interval of twelve months since the previous examination (or re-examination) had been completed. At a later period, in order to give additional encouragement to women to join the nursing classes, they were allowed to attend them immediately after the first aid course, without any interval, and reckoning them as first re-examination. More recently still the nursing course was opened to men, in response to a repeatedly expressed desire.

It was thought, and rightly so, that if a man or woman evinced sufficient interest in the work as to undergo these three examinations, there was little likelihood of their forgetting what they had been taught. From 1878 to 1897, 400,000 certificates and 51,000 medallions had been issued.[1]

If imitation be the sincerest form of flattery, the St. John Ambulance Association may certainly feel proud that its example should have been followed by Germany, and that a member of the Central Executive Committee, Mr. Furley, should have been invited to attend a meeting of the provisional committee at Kiel, at which the Samariter-Verein was originated, a Society which has not only spread over the whole of Germany, but has been closely copied in almost every State in Europe.

Mr. Furley visited Kiel in 1881, in order to assist at the preliminary meetings of a committee formed by Professor von Esmarch, an Honorary Associate of the Order, for the purpose of establishing an Ambulance Association, similar to that founded by the Order of St. John in England, in Germany. The German Association, called the "Deutscher Samariter-Verein," under the direct patronage and encour-

[1] The total number of certificates issued amounted to 535,000, and medallions 73,760.

THE AMBULANCE MOVEMENT 127

agement of the Empress of Germany, soon extended its operations from Kiel to Berlin. Prince Henry of Prussia accepted the office of Honorary President by the special desire of the Emperor. Other nations had been awakened to a sense of the value of Ambulance work in time of peace by the example of the Order of St. John in England. In Russia the very handbook used here, written by Dr. Shepherd, was translated for similar use, and in the United States the work was inaugurated in an earnest and businesslike spirit, and the Central Committee had great pleasure in affording the information and advice necessary. As before stated, large and numerous first-aid classes were formed in Germany by that distinguished Honorary Associate of the Order, Professor von Esmarch. His name had long been honoured in connection with ambulance work in war, but during a recent visit to England he was so much struck by what he saw of the St. John Ambulance Classes, that on his return to Germany he extended his energy and skill to ambulance work in general.

The incident thus related is most noteworthy. It brought the English Langue into a common development of work with the Teutonic brethren, and was the first step towards a real revival in Europe of the purposes and scope of the original Hospitallers; in spirit, if not literally, a return to the system by which the nations of the West were combined in a crusade of humanity towards their fellow-creatures, particularly in that Holy City whence all Christian charity derives its origin and inspiration. The influence and example of the English Langue, especially after the foundation of their hospital at Jerusalem, bore fruit in realizing this ideal as a practical purpose, and in this sustained effort for mankind we find our best title to the succession of those devoted pioneers of charity of whom Gerard was the first, although the progress of science and the advance of civilization may to some extent have altered both the field and the weapons of the humanitarian campaign.

> *Pro fide*, rang the war-cry of crusader,
>   Hewing his path through ranks of paynim foe.
> *Pro fide*, let us face the ghoule invader,
>   Dirt, drink, disease, the host of sin and woe :
> Faith will move mountains, once she life engrosses ;
>   Molehills of doubt the feeble onslaught baulk ;
> Power comes of courage—Victory with our cross is—
>   To do, not contemplate—to work, not talk.
> Spend and be spent for earth's self-helping sons.
> Thus cries the voice which issues from St. John's.[1]

The experience of a few years had proved that there could be no finality in the scheme of the Association. Thousands of men and women had been taught how to render first aid to the sick and injured. Centres of work had been formed in every part of the United Kingdom, and even in India and the Colonies. But the supply of pupils, especially in

[1] "Egeria," 1898.

THE AMBULANCE MOVEMENT 129

sparsely populated districts, could not always be maintained, and those who had received certificates and medallions exhibited great anxiety to maintain the position of their centres as spheres of daily usefulness. How was this to be done? An example was set at St. John's Gate by the establishment of a Corps for the transport of sick and injured patients, infectious cases excepted, and this new departure derived much encouragement from the gift made by a member of the Order of a completely fitted ambulance wagon. The Transport Corps was originally designed for the benefit of the poor, but the advantages it offered soon brought it to the notice of the more wealthy, who were not slow to avail themselves of its services. Thus it was anticipated that a double benefit would be secured, and that the new organization would be made self-supporting.

In 1885, the second year of the existence of this branch, 129 invalids, belonging to every class of society, availed themselves of the services of the new Corps, and the journeys ranged in length from one to two hundred miles. Up to the present time the register of cases shows 6,052 journeys, and many of these have extended to all parts of the Continent.

This example was followed in a modified form in other places. It was not possible, or even desirable, that other centres should organize Transport Corps of a similar character, but it was much to be wished that Corps for exclusively local requirements should be formed. A small beginning was made with Corps of eight men, and these were soon followed by others with larger and more ambitious aims; to these were added Nursing Corps of women who had received lessons in first-aid, supplemented by instruction in sick nursing which soon made them of great value to the doctors, more particularly in the mining and manufacturing districts.

Another branch of work which in a short time became very popular was the establishment of ambulance stations at national and international exhibitions, and at other places where large crowds assemble. Such stations were placed in the charge of one paid attendant (generally a retired soldier from the Army Medical Corps), assisted by volunteer ambulancers and supplemented by a local medical officer who could be readily summoned in case of serious emergency. Although several of such stations had been previously organized, the most important of the early stations was at the Colonial and Indian Exhibition in 1886. At this station 701 cases were treated, and 41 of these were removed in vehicles supplied by the Association. There were two deaths. In the same year 248 cases were received at the ambulance station in the International Exhibition of Liverpool. In the following year similar stations were established at the American Exhibition, Earl's Court, the Royal Military Tournament, and the Anglo-Danish Exhibition, South Kensington.

THE AMBULANCE MOVEMENT

A memorial to Colonel Francis Duncan, C.B., M.P., who will always be remembered for his services towards the initiation and establishment of the St. John Ambulance Association, called the Duncan Memorial Station, was placed in 1898 in the churchyard of St. Clement Danes, and tended night and day. This was removed in 1901 to the West India Docks; and a similar station, established by permission of the Dean and Chapter, at the expense of Dr. Edwin Freshfield, under the steps at the west end of St. Paul's Cathedral, was useful in the first twelve months to 203 people, and 2,296 cases have been treated there since it was opened.

The railway centres were found by experience to work quite to the satisfaction of the Directors, and received every encouragement from them; and on the occasion of a presentation of medallions, etc., in 1897, to the employés of the Great Western Railway, the Chairman, Lord Emlyn, stated that 3,714 had obtained certificates in the last decade, and that more than 800 cases had been treated by the company's servants during the last year. In the colliery and mining centres work constantly went on steadily and progressively, and an ambulance station has formed part of the establishment of each Annual Show of the Royal Agricultural Society since 1887. In the Colonies, and especially in Australia, work is still carried on with increased vigour, and the total issue of certificates by the Association in the twelve months of 1897 was 402,124.

In order to celebrate her late Majesty's Diamond Jubilee, three ambulance competitions were organized:
1. General, open to all centres and branches.
2. Railway, open to all Railways in England and Wales.
3. Brigade, open to all Corps and Divisions of the St. John Ambulance Brigade.

In number one the country was divided into eighteen districts, in which the preliminary heats were judged. The winners in each district then competed in five groups, the winners in which were finally judged at the Crystal Palace on the 6th May, the Dublin team being placed first.

In the Railway Division fifteen of the great companies competed, and at the final stage at the Crystal Palace the victory fell to the Great Eastern Railway; and in the Brigade competition of five teams the St. John's Gate team was judged the best.

Her late Majesty the Queen, the Sovereign Head and Patron of the Order, was graciously pleased to confer the distinction of Knighthood on Mr. John Furley, formerly Director of the Ambulance Department, Honorary Director of Stores, and Deputy Chairman of the St. John Ambulance Association (the Ambulance Department of the Order), of which he was one of the original founders.

The services of Sir John Furley, one of the oldest Knights of Justice in the Order, and a life member —*honoris causâ*—of the Central Executive Com-

THE CHALLENGE SHIELD.

THE AMBULANCE MOVEMENT 133

mittee, as a Commissioner for Sick and Wounded in War during several campaigns, and his equally zealous labours in time of peace for nearly forty years in the promotion of what is known as the Red Cross movement, have rendered his reputation European; while the invaluable stimulus given to the Ambulance Department by his experience, especially in connection with the invention and manufacture of material, can never be too highly estimated. This recognition of Sir John Furley's life-work, therefore, afforded the utmost satisfaction to his *confrères* in the Order, as well as amongst all those, both on the Continent and at home, who had been associated with him in the furtherance of a great national and humanitarian work which had received scant public attention before the institution of the Convention of Geneva.

By the creation of the Central British Red Cross Committee, under regulations approved by the Secretary of State for War, an object was obtained for which Sir John Furley had been working for a period of some thirty years. This Committee consists of representatives of the National Aid Society for the Sick and Wounded in War (which was initiated by the Order), of the St. John Ambulance Association, of the nursing Army reserve, and of the Secretary of State for War. On the outbreak of the South African War in 1899, Lord Knutsford and Sir John Furley represented the St. John

Ambulance Association. By the regulations of the Central British Red Cross Committee the Association was intrusted, *inter alia*, with two special branches of work—the collection and despatch to the seat of war of ambulance material and the organization of *personnel*.

With regard to the first of these, a great firm lent not only their warehouse, but the services of their staff. A member of the Order conducted the correspondence, and generally supervised the proceedings under the advice of the Chief Secretary, Sir Herbert Perrott. Vast quantities of material of all kinds were sent by the Castle line at special rates for the use of the sick and wounded, and distributed for a short time by Colonel Young, and later by Sir John Furley, both of whom at different times acted as Commissioner in South Africa.[1]

The appeal to the public for warm clothing and comforts of all kinds met with a most generous response, the various centres of the Association more particularly vieing with each other in the quantity and excellence of the comforts for the sick and wounded, and the method of packing.

Not only did members of the Royal Family and numbers of distinguished persons send contributions, but quantities of humble but useful gifts came from the poorer classes : *e.g.*, a pair of hand-knitted stock-

---

[1] See Report by Col. Richard Holbeche, presented to the Order, 1900.

THE AMBULANCE MOVEMENT 135

ings, a pair of gloves, a pipe, etc. These were often accompanied by pathetic letters.

The second object, the organization of *personnel* by the St. John Ambulance Brigade, is described elsewhere.

While furnishing the Central British Red Cross Committee with material and *personnel*, the item of the "sinews of war" had not been overlooked, and the Association forwarded a sum of £7,370 in cash, collected from its centres, branches, and supporters. Included in this sum were over £1,000 from the Middlesbrough-on-Tees and Cleveland centre, and £81 collected by the ladies of Peterborough entirely in shillings and pence, and £30 from a "Well Wisher" in Germany.

THE INDIAN BRANCH

Mr. Kennett Barrington proceeded to India as early as 1883 and arranged for the formation of centres in Calcutta and Bombay, with the cordial approval of the Governor of Bombay, the Lieutenant-Governor of Bengal, the Bishop of Calcutta, and many members of the British and native community. A class of native police had already been under instruction, and Princess Christian's translation of Dr. von Esmarch's handbook was re-translated into Mahariti for their benefit. Occasional classes were held in many places, but it was not till the year 1901 that the Indian branch of the Association was inaugurated on a basis which promises, if duly supported by the Government of India, to be permanent. The scheme laid before the Central Executive Committee by Major A. C. Yate in July, 1900, and subsequently expanded into a pamphlet, which was published at Calcutta in March, 1901, under the title of " Ambulance Work in India," aimed at a permanent organization on definite lines. That scheme advocated the establishment of centres all over India, in cities and cantonments, in native states, on the railways, and in the dockyards, among the police and volunteers, in connection with mines and factories, and in universities, colleges, and schools; and from the men and women trained by those centres it proposed to form an Ambulance and Nursing Brigade, as well as Bearer and Transport Corps. The appointment of Major Yate as Honorary Organizing Commissioner for India was sanctioned by the Grand Prior in December, 1900. The proposals made by Viscount Knutsford to the Viceroy of India, Lord Curzon of Kedleston, were favourably received; and, aided by the support of his authority, by the goodwill of the entire Press of India, European and native, and by the active help of many zealous and capable workers, Major Yate was able between the 20th of February and the 9th of May to start centres under favourable auspices at Calcutta, Madras, Bombay, Quetta, and Baroda. His health then obliged him to return to England.

THE AMBULANCE MOVEMENT 137

All things considered, good progress has been made in India during the past year. Calcutta has held thirteen classes of instruction, with an average attendance of twenty-seven, two or three of their classes being for Mahommedans. In January, 1902, the Lieutenant-Governor of Bengal presented 200 certificates to successful students. The Madras and Bombay centres, under the presidency of Lords Ampthill and Northcote, have done equally well. Some eight or ten of the principal railway companies in India have commenced to instruct their employés in first aid. The committees of the several centres are composed of enlightened and influential Hindus, Mahommedans, and Parsees, as well as Europeans; and natives of all three classes, including a small number of females, have undergone instruction. At Baroda everything has been left in the hands of the Gaikwar, who himself visited St. John's Gate in 1900. Classes of instruction have also been held at Simla, Duriagar, and Rawal Pundi, and among the Boer prisoners at Umbala. Both the First Aid and Nursing Manuals have been translated into Gujarati, and published with illustrations by Dr. Dhanjithai Melita, one of the Gaikwar's medical officers. Dr. Tukes, of the Church Missionary Society, has translated the First Aid Manual into Hindustani.

The latest reports show that the vitality of ambulance work in India is strong. With its population of nearly 300 millions, its army of a quarter of a million, its revenue of £90,000,000, and its import and export trade of £135,000,000, it affords the three things indispensable to success—men, women, and money. The other factors needed are initiation and a modicum at least of official recognition and support. Given these, the St. John Ambulance Association promises to become in India, in the space of a few years, what it already is in Great Britain and the Colonies, a very present help in time of peace and a godsend in war.

Auberge d'Angleterre

CHAPTER IX

THE CHARTER OF THE ENGLISH ORDER

THE first step towards a genuine revival of Hospitaller work in England was taken when the members of the Order removed their headquarters to the Gate of the ancient Priory of Clerkenwell, which had been secured for their use by the foresight of Sir Edmund Lechmere. As a *dilettante* charitable association, with chivalric traditions indeed, but only occupying temporary apartments under a roof which was not its own, an element of uncertainty pervaded both its inner organization and its external work; but the very *genius loci* of the old headquarters of the English Langue seemed to breathe its inspiration into the proceedings of the Council under its own roof, and steady progress has since marked its history.

It is true that not until 1887 was a company formed, consisting of members of the Order alone, for the acquisition of the freehold of St. John's Gate; but for ten years previously to that date the whole of the vast machinery of first-aid classes, examinations, and certificates, in all its ramifications at home and abroad, had been directed from the headquarters at Clerkenwell.

The rapid growth of this movement was due to the fact that the conviction among those of higher educational attainments that ambulance work had become a serious study of real importance, not an amusement to be taken up and dropped at pleasure, was insensibly causing a more elevated standard of proficiency to be required, thus imperatively demanding a central management. The white eight-pointed cross of the Order, surrounded by the words "St. John Ambulance Association," furnished an official symbol of this conviction, and became the recognized badge of centres and of classes wherever formed.

That these continually increased was in no small degree owing to the kind feeling towards the Association evinced by the members of the medical profession. The ambulance pupil had his position clearly defined, and was taught never to cross the line which separates him from the province of the trained medical man. In the metropolis, as well as in the provinces, hospitals were often placed at the disposal of the classes by the kindness and public spirit of the Governors. In London, for instance, the hospitals of King's College and St. Thomas, and others, were so used.

Sir Edward Sieveking, a Knight of Grace, one of the most earnest supporters of the Order from his admission as an Honorary Associate in 1869, in 1887 presided over a meeting of hospital physicians and surgeons, including many leading members of the profession, held at St. John's Gate, where expressions of approval and resolutions were unanimously passed, urging that every effort should be made to make known, far and wide, the able work being done in a direction where the general practitioner so often finds the resources at his disposal fall far short of that standard which the comfort and well-being of the patient demand.

This gradually became a national work, and the nation realized the fact that the spirit of the old motto of the Order—*Infirmis servire, firmissimum regnare*—was perpetuated by the doings of this new society, which speedily attracted the patronage of the highest in the land.

First of the Royal Family to appreciate (with that delicate instinct for charity which has ever been one of her most gracious characteristics) the good which was being quietly done, our present Queen, then Princess of Wales, became a Lady of the Order in 1876, and since that date it has received the support and countenance of almost every member of the Royal House, several of whom, as the late Duke of Albany in 1883, were formally received into the ranks of the Order. Had the life of his Royal Highness the Duke of Albany been prolonged, he would doubtless have taken an active share in the proceedings of the Order, as was done by the Duke of Connaught (Bailiff of Eagle) and the late Duke of Clarence, the first Sub-Prior under the new Charter. But the Princesses who wore the cross of the Order had not adopted it in a spirit of patronage only; the late Duchess of Teck, the Princess Christian, Princess Henry of Battenberg, and other royal ladies not merely presented certificates and assisted at public meetings, but personally attended classes and qualified as skilled holders of certificates of proficiency.

The usefulness of the system became more and more evident, not only at home but abroad. During the Egyptian War it was through the exertions of its members that the Victoria Hospital at Cairo was the means of relieving the sufferings of many of the unfortunate Arab soldiers, and also of saving the lives of several British officers. An effort was made to perpetuate this connection with the Order of St. John by calling it the St. John's Hospital, but the Khedive preferred an appellation better comprehensible by an Oriental and named it after her late Majesty Queen Victoria.

It is interesting, in connection with this subject, to notice that immediately after the insurrection at Alexandria numbers of refugees fled to Malta, where at that time Lady Houlton had just introduced the ambulance work. It was the hottest period of the year; over 1,200 families, of from four to six persons each, were thrown on the charity of the island; but

CHARTER OF ENGLISH ORDER 143

the ladies of the Order and their friends, assisted by the Mansion House Committee, provided clothing, bedding, and other necessary support for the refugees in so complete a manner as to call forth the acknowledgments of the Government at home.

The success of the beneficent work of the Order at Jerusalem must form the subject of another chapter.

The Order during these years of progress had to lament the loss of several of its most valued and useful *confrères*. In 1877 the Order sustained a very serious loss by the death of its Registrar, Richard Woolfe. He had devoted himself to the interests of the Order with zeal and energy; by his will he bequeathed to the Order the sum of £1,000, in aid of the charitable purposes of the Order, and also his books and papers relating to the Order. A resolution was passed at the first Chapter after his death placing upon record its deep sense of the great loss which the Order had sustained. A memorial, consisting of an engraved brass, was designed, with a view to its being erected in the crypt of St. John's Church.

We may pass over many worthy and distinguished names, but one requires especial mention.

In March, 1887, the Order of St. John and the cause of philanthropy generally sustained a great loss by the death of Viscountess Strangford, which took place on her voyage to Port Said. Since her admission to the Order in 1873, there was hardly a single Hospitaller object of importance to which Lady Strangford had not devoted her experiences and her energy, making herself the very pattern of a Dame Chevalière. She took a deep interest in hospital nursing, and went through a course of training in one of the principal London hospitals. She greatly aided a committee of the Order in their successful efforts to draw the attention of the public to the want of better nurses for the working classes at their own homes, and the establishment of the National Association for providing nurses for the sick poor was the result. The Bulgarian Relief Fund of nearly £30,000 was raised by her own efforts, and expended under her direction with the assistance of Sir V. Kennett Barrington. In 1877 Lady Strangford formed a fund for the relief of the Turkish sick and wounded in the Turco-Russian War. She went with her staff of nurses to the front, and there opened and maintained her hospitals. In the course of the war she was taken prisoner by the Russians, and underwent hardships from which she never fully recovered. In 1882 she proceeded at the request of the St. John Ambulance Association to Cairo, and established and opened the Victoria Hospital for the relief of the sick and wounded, and many English officers and soldiers owe their lives to the tender care and skilful nursing there obtained. On her return Queen

CHARTER OF ENGLISH ORDER 145

Victoria conferred on her the distinction of the Red Cross Order. Her last effort, the visit to Port Said, undertaken to fulfil a promise, proved fatal. Thus closed a life in which everything—money, health, and energy—had been freely lavished in the cause of self-sacrifice and devotion to duty, of which she was so striking an example.

No doubt there were other branches of work carried on at home which developed the circle of beneficent assistance to the needy: the Almoner's department in London, and the Hanley Castle Commandery, under the especial care of Sir Edmund Lechmere, provided nourishing "diets" of food for the convalescents discharged from hospitals or recommended by clerical and medical adherents of the Order. But throughout these years the great progress made in first-aid instruction was the prominent feature of the work of the Order, not only among ladies and men of leisure, but in the navy, the army, the police force and railway servants, in mines, in collieries, and in every scene of laborious industry. Indeed among the denser industrial populations a missionary propaganda was established, and an ambulance crusade in the Northumberland and Durham coal-fields was undertaken by Surgeon-Major George Hutton, during the period between September 23rd and November 2nd, 1888. During this tour Surgeon-Major Hutton attended meetings and delivered addresses at twenty-four colliery towns and villages, besides holding innumerable interviews and arranging the preliminaries for classes; and so satisfactory were the results that he was requested by the Committee to inaugurate the forthcoming autumn session by another and still more extended expedition in the northern counties. These measures received the hearty approbation of the mining authorities in the Durham and Northumberland districts. This development of work became more imperative after the passing of the Mines Regulation Act, which came into operation on January 1st, 1887. It was a feature also of this period of great public exhibitions, like the Colonial and Indian, the Liverpool and others, to undertake the establishment of Ambulance Stations on such occasions at all places where large crowds might be expected to assemble.

The streets of the metropolis had already experienced the usefulness of the Ambulance Corps from St. John's Gate on such occasions as the annual City procession on Lord Mayor's Day, but it was at the various processions and festivals which in 1887 marked the national rejoicing on the occasion of Queen Victoria's Jubilee that their presence became an integral part of the public precautions for the safeguard of the populace. The absolute necessity for an ambulance service in connection with the Metropolitan Police being then fully recognized, the Chief Commissioner personally took part in and

CHARTER OF ENGLISH ORDER

encouraged the efforts which were made by the Ambulance Corps in co-operatiou with the police.

Thus the useful teaching of first aid had spread to all classes of the community. No grade was unrepresented : royal personages, servants and workwomen, soldiers, sailors, mechanics, policemen, railway guards and porters, miners, in fact all sorts and conditions of men thronged to the classes, passed the same examinations, and worked for the same certificates and medallions.

In 1888 the system was ripe for that recognition which her late Majesty was always prompt to give to every institution of public benefit, and from her royal hand the Order received its Charter as the Grand Priory of the Order of the Hospital of St. John of Jerusalem in England, the St. John Ambulance Association being incorporated with it as one of its principal departments, and made subject to its laws and regulations.

The Charter will be given elsewhere, but the fact that his present Majesty (then Prince of Wales) accepted the position of Grand Prior is a gratifying testimony to the energy and ability with which the necessary arrangements for obtaining this Royal recognition were conducted by Mr. Amherst (Lord Amherst of Hackney).

The installation of H.R.H. as Grand Prior, which opened a new era in the history of English Hospitaller work, took place at St. John's Gate, August, 1888.

By his constant and judicious supervision of the general operations of the Order, the Grand Prior soon made his royal influence felt in every department of its work as a stimulus to exertion. In especial by personally conferring the medal instituted by the Order in 1874 as a reward for deeds of gallantry in saving life on land, and graciously inviting to Marlborough House the male and female recipients of this distinction, the Grand Prior gave to the decoration a value which it had not before enjoyed. Twice has St. John's Gate had the honour of a visit from its royal chief: at his Installation in 1889; and again in 1893, when the loss which the Order had sustained by the decease of the first Sub-Prior, H.R.H. the Duke of Clarence, was commemorated by a tablet of arms placed upon the City face of the archway after its renovation.

DUKE OF CLARENCE MEMORIAL TABLET

CHAPTER X

OPHTHALMIC HOSPITAL IN JERUSALEM

THE English branch of the Order of St. John of Jerusalem had for some time after their revival been considering the advisability of establishing a Hospice and Ophthalmic Dispensary at Jerusalem, to meet a long-standing and acknowledged want, and to gain the wished-for *pied à terre* in the Holy City. In December, 1876, Sir Edmund Lechmere, then its secretary, presented a memorandum on behalf of the Order to Sir Henry Elliot, our Minister at Constantinople, asking that a site in the city of Jerusalem might be given on which to erect an English hospital, and this memorandum was presented to the Porte. The site which the Order desired was not available; much delay therefore was occasioned. Later, Mr. Noel Moore, H.B.M. Consul in Jerusalem, found a suitable site, and Sir A. Layard communicated with the Porte, but an answer was received to the effect that an expression of opinion was awaited from the Governor of the Holy Places. Lord Salisbury interested himself in the matter, and Sir Philip Cunliffe brought the object of the Chapter to the notice of H.R.H. the Prince of Wales, who at once expressed his desire to aid in promoting its success, and conveyed through the Turkish Ambassador in England his personal request that a site might be granted; consequently a memorandum explaining the wishes of the Chapter was transmitted to Musurus Pasha.

This representation bore fruit, for a year later the Order had the satisfaction of hearing that the Sultan had granted a Firman conceding a site at Jerusalem for a hospice of the Order, to include a dispensary for ophthalmic cases. The following report from the Jerusalem Hospice Committee appointed in 1881 was presented to the Chapter:

"It is now just one year since the request of the Order for a grant of land on which to erect a British Hospice, and a Dispensary for the treatment of cases of Ophthalmia was made to the Ottoman Government, supported by the personal interest of H.R.H. the Prince of Wales. The result of that request cannot be better told than by the publication of the Firman of the 24th of April, 1882, received by the Committee from the Porte through the Turkish Ambasssador in London on the 23rd May, 1882.

"FIRMAN

"To Raouf Pasha, my Noble Governor of the Sandjak of Jerusalem, bearer of my Imperial Orders of the Medjidije of the Second Class and of the Osmanieh of the Fourth Class.

HOSPICE AT JERUSALEM.
From the Report of 1883.

OPHTHALMIC HOSPITAL

"On the arrival of my Imperial Emblem be it known to you that the British Embassy has reported and requested as follows:

"The Prince of Wales, son of the Queen of England, manifested the wish that my Imperial Government should be pleased to concede as a gift a piece of ground of ten thousand square 'zirae' approximately for the establishment by the English members of the Society of St. John at Jerusalem of a Hospice and a place for tending gratuitously poor invalids.

"Such an establishment being one of public utility, it was decided in my council of Ministers that a piece of ground of the extent required should be granted in the same manner and under the same conditions (as?) the one which was previously granted there to the Prince of Prussia for the foundation of a similar establishment by the German branch of the said Society, and at a place free of all local objections; upon this, my Imperial sanction having been besought, I was pleased to grant it and to convey it through this my noble Firman emanating from my Imperial Divan, and delivered to whom it may concern.

"You, therefore, who are the above-mentioned Governor, have to provide for the required piece of ground of ten thousand 'zirae' approximately, and one which may not give rise to local objections, and to show and offer the said ground to the aforesaid English Society, while taking care that it should be employed in the manner and under conditions identical to those under which the grant of such a piece of ground to the German branch of the Society was previously made.

"1299 Djemazil Lakhir 5 (24th April, 1882)."

This concession was a subject for congratulation, not only to the Order, but also far beyond the circle of its own interests, as it was likely to assist materially the humanitarian and charitable object they had in view.

The property thus acquired is situated on the Bethlehem Road, about eight minutes' walk from the Jaffa Gate, and is some six acres in extent. On one side it is bounded by the Valley of Hinnom, on the other by the Bethlehem Road. The hospital stands at the west end and narrowest part of the ground; it is extremely well built of the best materials, contains eighteen chambers, and has an abundant water-supply.

In order to show the need that existed for such an establishment, the testimony of a few distinguished persons may be quoted.

Mrs. Burton, authoress of "The Inner Life of Syria, Palestine and the Holy Land," wrote to Sir Edmund Lechmere: "I do not know any greater charity that any one or any institution could do for Syria than to start something which might one day become an eye hospital. Nowhere are there such beautiful eyes, and nowhere so eaten up with dirt and disease, with-

OPHTHALMIC HOSPITAL

out hope or remedy, as in Syria. A good English oculist would be God's own blessing out there: the whole country would swarm to him. The disease begins from birth, with dirt, neglect, flies and sun. You will find old people's eyes, say at fifty, gone incurably. Youths and girls may still be saved, and parents trained to wash the babies' eyes, and keep the flies off which settle on offal, and then on the eyes, and no one drives them away."

Sir Austin Layard wrote: "I have no hesitation in saying that an hospital at Jerusalem for persons suffering from affection of the eye would be a very valuable institution. I am not aware whether there exists at the present time any place where the poor can obtain gratuitous advice and aid in cases of eye disease. . . . Diseases of the eye are so common in Syria and Palestine that I cannot conceive any charitable institution that would confer greater benefit on the poor than one that will deal with a malady which has such painful and distressing effects."

William Bowman, Esq., F.R.S., the eminent oculist, writing to the same in June, 1882, said: "It is most kind of you to have written to me about the Order of St. John and their excellent project at Jerusalem, there being no doubt whatever that untold misery results from the inherent and wellnigh incredible filth, squalor, indolence and ignorance of sanitary laws pervading almost the whole population of those Levantine countries.

Such an hospital would be a centre of remedial and preventative influences, and I most cordially wish it success."

On Friday, 7th July, 1882, a meeting in furtherance of this charitable work at Jerusalem was held at the Jerusalem Chamber, Westminster Abbey, under the presidency of the Earl of Shaftesbury, when the following resolution was adopted :

"That this meeting cordially approves of the proposal made by the English Langue of the Order of St. John to establish a British Hospice and Ophthalmic Dispensary at Jerusalem : and recognizing their object as being at once humanitarian and national, recommends it to the hearty support of the public."

Among the speakers on this occasion were Sir Edmund Lechmere, M.P., Sir Richard Temple, Colonel Duncan, Mr. Tyssen Amherst, M.P. (now Lord Amherst of Hackney), Dr. Thomas Chaplin (of Jerusalem), the Bishop of Gibraltar, General Viscount Templetown, and others.

The result of the meeting was to arouse to some extent outside sympathy and help, and this and the generosity of Lady Lechmere enabled the Order to appoint a medical officer and begin work. Dr. Waddell, who was selected, left for Jerusalem in November, and, having secured temporary premises, began the beneficent work of the Order on the 4th December, 1882, and six months after was able to report that the number of patients had been 1,952,

OPHTHALMIC HOSPITAL 155

while the total of those who had received advice and medicine was 6,138. On many days the attendance reached the large number of 140. Shortly after arrangements for the conveyance of the site by H.I.M. the Sultan were made, and a large house on it obtained by purchase. A Turkish regulation required hospitals at Jerusalem to be attached to a specific church to enable them to receive drugs, etc., free of import duty. Application was made by H.B.M. *Chargé d'Affaires* at Constantinople to obtain the privilege directly to the Order, and the work at Jerusalem so commended itself to the Sublime Porte that notification was made that the privilege of receiving medical stores free of duty had been granted in favour of the hospice and dispensary belonging to the English branch of the Order of St. John of Jerusalem. In order to help to raise a large sum a concert, under the patronage of the Prince and Princess of Wales and all the Royal Family, was given in Grosvenor House, which had been lent by the Duke of Westminster. Regulations for the management of the hospice were drawn up in 1883, and among other items it was determined that the immediate control of the hospital should be intrusted to a local committee, that an honorary consulting surgeon should be appointed, that the general management of the affairs of the hospital should be conducted by a general committee of members and associates meeting at the headquarters of the Order at its Chancery, St. John's Gate, Clerkenwell, London, and having for its executive officers a chairman, a vice-chairman, a treasurer, and two honorary secretaries, to be aided in all medical and surgical matters relating to the working of the hospital by a medical sub-committee. As the hospital and dispensary were intended solely for the poor, it was ordered that those who were admitted as patients, and were able to aid its funds, should do so at the discretion of the surgeon, after investigation and reference to the local committee.

Arrangements were now made for the reception of in-patients, and beginning in a small way four beds were constantly occupied, mostly with cases requiring surgical aid. Thirty-nine major and several minor operations were performed, nearly all being successful. More beds were greatly needed, however, as patients had frequently to be refused admission for diseases which could only be successfully treated in hospital, and thus many poor people lost the chance of being completely cured. The patients belonged to all the various faiths which prevailed in Jerusalem, and as their religious opinions were in no way interfered with, all came freely into the dispensary and hospital. The news that it had been opened was spreading around, and already patients were coming from such far distant places as Jaffa, Gaza, Tiberias, and from the desert beyond Jordan and the Dead Sea. It was, however, considered wise first to place the hospital on a sound business foundation before greatly extending it.

In November, 1886, Sir Edmund and Lady Lechmere visited the hospital and found it in excellent order. The Governor of Jerusalem, the Orthodox Greek Patriarch, the Armenian Patriarch, and the Chief Rabbi paid them visits of ceremony. Raouf Pasha, the Governor, continued to take a lively interest in the hospital, and the Chief Rabbi presented a memorial in Hebrew, which recorded the gratitude of the Jewish population, and "their confidence in the absence of any proselytising intention." The thanks of the Order were awarded to his Beatitude the Greek Patriarch, and to Mr. Ogilvie, the resident surgeon of the hospital. Three thousand and twelve new patients had been treated at the dispensary, and one hundred and twenty-four admitted to the hospital.

Sir Edmund described how, although most of the patients came from the immediate neighbourhood of Jerusalem, many travelled from considerable distances; some from as far as Nablous in Samaria; and that all seemed willing to submit to any amount of trouble and fatigue in order to obtain the aid of the English eye doctor. He concludes with the following reflections, which may well be quoted :

"And may not we of the Order of St. John venture to hope that as the work of our original Founders commenced with a hospital at Jerusalem, and became in time one of the greatest institutions in Christendom; so the Langue of England, which has once more resumed its connection with the earliest home of the Order, may receive an additional blessing from its philanthropic labours."

His Royal Highness the Prince of Wales, after expressing his pleasure at the work done in the hospice, gave it his patronage.

In 1888 Dr. Ogilvie reported that in the previous three and a half years upwards of 10,000 patients had been treated, and the number of consultations had approached 58,000. When the work began it was regarded with suspicion by the people, who were intensely conservative; but in course of time, when they found that their religion was in no way interfered with, they came by degrees to the just conclusion that it was their interest alone which was studied, and in the following year Dr. Cant, who had succeeded Dr. Ogilvie as Medical Superintendent, gave the numbers of persons who had been treated as 7,623, and operations as 324, showing how much the work of the supporters of the charity was being appreciated. The number of beds had been increased to sixteen, including two endowed beds, one supported by the orthodox Greek Patriarch of Jerusalem, the other by the Right Reverend the Anglican Bishop of Jerusalem. They were always full, 219 in-patients having been admitted, these very often having come considerable distances extending over a district of more than 100 miles in length, from Nazareth in the north to the district of Gaza southward, and from the sea-coast on the west to beyond Jordan and the Dead Sea. The patients were in the main taken from two classes, Jews, mostly from Jerusalem itself, and Arabs, Fellaheen from the various towns and villages in the district described.

The high degree in which the hospital was appreciated was abundantly shown by the number of applicants for relief, a number in 1890 greatly in excess of the resources either of the out-patient or in-patient department, and continually increasing, so that it frequently happened that the door had to be closed soon after daybreak, and that applicants amounting to many hundreds were refused owing to lack of accommodation and surgical assistance. Two nurses were at this period despatched from England. In this year the number of new cases was 3,757 and the total attendance 9,468, which in the following year rose to 12,881. In the Jubilee year a present was made to the hospital by Queen Victoria, the Sovereign Head and Patron of the Order, of a portrait of herself, which was duly accorded a place of honour, and caused the greatest interest and admiration among the patients. The increase of work that marked 1897 was so great that it brought into prominence the inability of the hospital to cope with the requirements of the population of the city and surrounding country, and the necessity for some change so as to keep the number of patients within limits. The doors were opened early in the morning of each out-patient day, and were closed as soon as patients in sufficient numbers to afford full occupation for the day had been admitted. As soon as this was known the people came earlier and earlier until a crowd often assembled during the night; hence the residents benefited more by the charity than did the afflicted more distant villages. In 1893 a new out-patient block was built in memory of General Gordon, generously helped by Miss Wilson, the late Sir Edmund Lechmere, and Mr. John A. Cook; and an assistant surgeon to Dr. Cant, who succeeded Dr. Ogilvie, appointed to meet the overwhelming pressure of the out-patient department. The good effects of this were immediately apparent, and the work of the hospital was accomplished through the busy season in a manner which left little to be desired.

The hospital annually receives large numbers of people suffering from actual or impending blindness; and as it is practically the only one to which they can apply, not the least part of its good work is in furnishing a common ground on which the Christian, the Jew and the Mahommedan meet upon equal terms, and learn to entertain sentiments of goodwill and mutual respect for one another.

The following letter speaks for itself:

"Jerusalem,
"September 28th, 1901.

"I am glad that the Order of St. John has been able to give great prominence to the Ophthalmic Hospital, of which you are Chairman. It is doing excellent work, and it is known and trusted throughout the country, and even to Moab and the trans-Jordan country.

"Dr. Cant's name is one of note here. He performed an operation for cataract on me last year, quite painlessly and quite successfully. I must have resigned otherwise, but I can now see forty miles of distance and read 'diamond type.' I heard of him in England as one of the first men of the day, to whom anything might have been open at home. I only got the same attention that he gave to an old bedridden woman who was his patient before me. He is in every way a good man, but very retiring.

"The work of the hospital is sometimes spoken against because it is not directly missionary. But it is known far and wide as the work of charity and philanthropy by men who do the work for the sake of Christ. It is neither mixed up with proselytism (as our missions have been much) nor with politics (as foreign institutions are), but it has done a fine work in breaking down prejudice, and it is real and thorough. The new building will be a great advantage.

162 HOSPITALLERS OF ST. JOHN

"It is well that the ancient Order should have its hospital here, accessible to all, and free. It has greatly subdued the worst forms of eye disease, as people now understand that their sight can be saved if they go in time.

"(Signed) G. W. BLYTH,
"Bishop in Jerusalem."

This testimony was submitted to his Majesty, the Supreme Head and Patron of the Order, and to H.R.H. the Grand Prior, and both were graciously pleased to express their satisfaction at receiving such a report.

There is no doubt that the Order has acted wisely and well in establishing its hospital, as of old, on an unsectarian basis. It has taken a most important step in forwarding civilization, as by extending the benefits of the institution to all alike, without interfering with or even referring to religious views, it brings the blessings and the good effects of civilization prominently before the people themselves and so induces them to adopt it.

In 1901 the generous gift of £1,000 by an anonymous benefactor for the enlargement of the building permitted the commencement of work which will place the hospital upon an extended basis, and will allow the number of beds to be increased to forty; and numbers of persons will be admitted and cured who at present cannot fail to suffer seriously

OPHTHALMIC HOSPITAL 163

from the combined effects of long journeys and imperfect nursing at home.

It will be seen that the hospital arose chiefly on the initiation of Sir Edmund Lechmere, and its early maintenance devolved greatly upon his liberality, as well as upon that of Lord Amherst of Hackney, Mr. John M. Cook being a generous helper; and to Lady Lechmere the hospital has throughout been greatly indebted, and owing to her exertions in conjunction with friends a supply of clothing has always been forthcoming, which has saved the hospital fund considerable expense. More than can be expressed also is due to the enthusiasm of Dr. and Mrs. Cant. Dr. Cant has been in residence for fourteen years, and during that period has treated 6,323 admitted patients, 175,725 out-patients, and has performed 13,294 operations, 6,752 of which have required anæsthetics.

An interesting table showing the growth of the usefulness and popularity of the institution will be found in an Appendix.

The hospital is supported by the voluntary contributions of members and associates of the Order and the general public, the people of Scotland being particularly generous, and Mr. A. A. Gordon, Knight of Grace of the Order of St. John and a member of H.M. Bodyguard of Scotland, has annually been able to forward a noble sum from that country in aid of the good work.

In the central hall of the hospital hangs a picture of the great Queen given by her Majesty herself, and a handsome tablet is erected to the pious memory of one at whose initiative the hospice was established, Sir Edmund Lechmere, Chancellor of the Order of St. John of Jerusalem in England.

CHAPTER XI

THE ST. JOHN AMBULANCE BRIGADE AND ITS SERVICES

THE assistance given in kind and money to the sick and wounded in South Africa by the St. John Ambulance Association has been recorded in a previous chapter, but a far greater duty was performed by the St. John Ambulance Brigade in rendering personal service at the seat of war. The Brigade is an offshoot of the parent Association, its distinguishing feature being that it is a voluntary organization for rendering first aid to the public in a systematic manner by members holding the certificate of the St. John Ambulance Association, whose efficiency is periodically tested. The Brigade works under the general supervision of the Ambulance Department of the Order of St. John, and is centrally controlled by the Chief Commissioner (Colonel Bowdler) at St. John's Gate, assisted by Deputy Commissioners, each of whom acts for a distinct and definite district. The details of the formation and discipline of local corps and divisions, which together form the Brigade, have been so far systematized that they form parts of one complete and harmonious whole, and the members are not only available for local purposes, but under certain conditions may volunteer to serve in case of national emergency.

The objects of the Brigade are thus defined in the General Regulations approved by the Council and Chapter of the Order of St. John:

1. To afford holders of first-aid certificates from the St. John Ambulance Association opportunities of meeting together for ambulance and nursing practice, with the object of combining individual efforts for the public advantage.

2. To render first aid to the sick and injured on public occasions, with the sanction of the police and other authorities, and to maintain in readiness for such duty a body of trained men and nurses qualified so to act.

3. To enroll a body of civilians, qualified in first aid and trained in ambulance drill or nursing duties, willing to be placed at the disposal of the military and other authorities as a supplement to the public medical services in case of necessity either at home or abroad.

4. To train men in ambulance transport duties.

5. To develop and promote every means of rendering aid to the injured.

A chapter upon the Brigade system would now be most incomplete without a reference to the circumstances which caused it, so to speak, to become, at

THE AMBULANCE BRIGADE 167

any rate during a critical period, an integral and essential part of our national defences. During the war in South Africa the Order, for the first time in its history, has had, through the Brigade, the privilege of contributing to the defence of the Empire, and the experiment has proved so successful that it is possible that, in the event of any future mobilization of the forces, its members may again be deemed eligible to supplement the ranks of the Royal Army Medical Corps.[1]

In 1898, it being foreseen that in case of national emergency the Brigade might be able to render valuable assistance to the naval and military authorities, negotiations were opened with the War Office with a view of arriving at some arrangement as regards the conditions under which members of the Brigade could be employed as auxiliaries to the Royal Army Medical Corps.

In February, 1899, a letter was addressed to the Secretary of State for War by the Chief Commissioner of the St. John Ambulance Association, suggesting that it would be well to arrange in time of peace the conditions under which, in case of mobilization of the army, the Brigade could be employed, and negotiations ensued as to the regulations to be adopted.

[1] The following details have been taken mainly from the Report of the Commissioner on the mobilization of the Brigade for service in South Africa.

In the meantime the gist of these conditions had been communicated to the Chief Commissioner, and on the 27th October, 1899, a preliminary confidential memorandum was issued by him to all corps and divisions, calling for a return of volunteers for service in South Africa. The Brigade was thus happily prepared for the first call of volunteers, which was received from the War Office on the 3rd of November. From that time forward, as the resources of the Army Medical Corps became more exhausted, continuous calls were made on the Brigade, and these were invariably met without any hesitation or delay.

It should be borne in mind that two distinct classes of contingents were furnished by the Brigade for service in South Africa: first, men required as auxiliaries to the Royal Army Medical Corps, for the Princess Christian (Mr. Moseley's) Hospital, and for the Rhodesian Field Hospital, all of whom served immediately under the War Office; second, men required for service in private hospitals equipped under the auspices of the Central British Red Cross Committee, with the sanction of the Director-General, Army Medical Service. Under this head are included the "Princess of Wales" hospital ship, the Portland Hospital, the Princess Christian Hospital Train, the American (Mr. Van Alen's) section of a field hospital, the Imperial Yeomanry Hospital, the Langman Hospital, the Imperial Yeomanry Field

THE AMBULANCE BRIGADE 169

Hospital, and the "Maine" (American) hospital ship, the men in which categories served under contract with the committees or providers of the hospitals.

It has been a source of great disappointment to a large number of the nursing officers and sisters of the Brigade that their services could not be utilized in South Africa. Many of them are thoroughly qualified for nursing duties in hospitals, but the supply of members of the Army Nursing Reserve has been so ample that no other nurses have been sent out from England by the War Office as a supplement to the Army Nursing Service.

Speaking generally, the routine of calling in volunteers was as follows. The conditions of service and the qualifications required of volunteers, being published in Brigade Orders, were made known to every member of the Brigade, and in each corps and division volunteers were called upon to give in their names to their officers and to pass the required medical examination, the latter being held by the honorary surgeons of their unit.

Blank forms of returns of volunteers for war service were printed and sent to each corps and division for completion and submission to Deputy Commissioners of Districts.

On receipt of a requisition for men from the War Office, or from the committee or provider of a hospital sanctioned by the War Office, the Deputy Commissioner of each of the six Brigade districts was directed by telegraph to report to Brigade headquarters the number of qualified volunteers at his disposal at the time. The quota to be furnished by his district was then communicated by telegram to each Deputy Commissioner, a week's notice being given whenever possible, before the men were required to assemble at Brigade headquarters. The dates of assembly in London were, as a rule, at least eight days before the approximate date of embarkation of the contingent, a clear week being necessary for the completion of the clothing and equipment of the men, and for their special instruction in nursing duties and drill.

It is to be observed that, in the case of each contingent called for, the quota of men ordered to be furnished by the several districts was calculated as nearly as possible in accordance with the proportion of men who had at the time of the call volunteered for service. This undoubtedly caused some little delay, as it necessitated waiting until every Deputy Commissioner had reported the number of men in hand, but the principle appeared to be sound; each district was allowed to furnish its due proportion of volunteers. Moreover, distinct directions were issued to the Deputy Commissioners that, in selecting their men, every division of the Brigade, however small, was, as far as possible, to have the chance of sending its fair proportion of representatives.

On joining at headquarters the men were at first

THE AMBULANCE BRIGADE 171

billeted only in certain inns in immediate proximity to St. John's Gate; but as this accommodation was not sufficient for the large contingents subsequently assembled, arrangements were made for quartering the majority of the men in an empty warehouse in St. John's Square, where they were provided with meals furnished by a contractor at the rate of about 3*s.* 6*d.* a day per man. The bedding for the men in barracks was obtained on requisition from the Commissariat Department. Of that required for the men quartered in the public-houses referred to, the Military Equipment Company (Waterloo Place) were good enough to lend twenty-three bedsteads and the necessary bedding for one month. On the withdrawal of this Messrs. Maple and Co. (Tottenham Court Road) very generously supplied fifty bedsteads and sets of bedding for a similar period.

The messing was on the whole very satisfactory, as but few well-grounded complaints were made. The sleeping accommodation of the men in barracks was not as comfortable as one could have wished; for, owing to the restricted space at disposal, bedsteads could not be provided, and the bedding consisted of coir paillasses, placed close together on the floor of the sleeping-rooms, and a sufficiency of blankets. Due precautions were taken to disinfect the rooms, and the health of the men, under rather adverse circumstances, was remarkably good, only two cases of serious illness having occurred.

But for the system of organization which already existed, it would have been impossible to gather from such distant and scattered sources a steady stream of recruits, and indeed the utmost energy was required to keep pace with the demand for men.

Some notion of the difficulties with which the Deputy Commissioners and Superintendents of corps and divisions throughout the country had to contend may be formed from the following considerations. In the first place, the men did not volunteer for the several contingents by complete units (corps or divisions), but individually, or in groups from the several divisions. Thus a Deputy Commissioner who was called upon to furnish sixty men on a certain date, or to hold them in readiness to join on an approximate date, might have to communicate with ten or twenty Superintendents of divisions in various parts of his district, and similarly the Superintendents would have at once to look up their quota of men, who might be living several miles apart. Again, considerations of expense and of the insufficiency of the headquarters staff made it impossible to keep up a permanent depot in London from which contingents could be drawn from time to time as required ; and even if such a depot could have been continuously maintained, it was manifestly out of the question to keep men on hand longer than was necessary in order to complete their outfit and

THE AMBULANCE BRIGADE 173

put them through a course of drill and instruction in nursing duties, seeing that under the War Office regulations they receive no pay prior to embarkation; consequently men were never called in until positive instructions had been received from the War Office, or private hospitals, that the men would be required to embark on a certain date, and these requisitions were often received very few days before it would be necessary to assemble the men in London. Further, as the dates of sailing of the transports which were to convey the several contingents were sometimes suddenly advanced or postponed several days, the men had frequently to be called in sooner or later than the day for which every one had been already warned. It will be gathered from these considerations that every one concerned—Chief Commissioner, Deputy Commissioners, Superintendents, and volunteers—lived in a constant state of suspense, and that in consequence there was an infinitely greater amount of correspondence, inconvenience, and strain involved in the mobilization of fifty or sixty men of the Brigade than would be necessitated by the removal of a battalion of soldiers.

As illustrations of the rapidity with which the calling in of the men was effected, the following instances may be mentioned. The order for the second contingent, fifty-five men, was received at headquarters on the morning of the 20th November, and before midnight of the 22nd the whole of the men from all parts of the kingdom were assembled at the Gate and fitted with clothing and fully equipped, although they did not embark until the 25th. Again, the order for eleven selected men suddenly required for the hospital ship "Maine" reached the Deputy Commissioner of No. 4 District at midnight on Saturday, 28th April. On Sunday nothing could be done, and yet the men reported themselves at St. John's Gate on Tuesday morning, were clothed and equipped, and embarked at Southampton by midday on Thursday, 3rd May. Perhaps the following is the most remarkable instance of rapid execution of orders that has occurred during the mobilization. Owing to the miscarriage of a telegram, the order for sixty-six men of No. 4 District to join at headquarters on the 8th May was not received by the Deputy Commissioner. A second telegram which was despatched to him on the night of the 10th May reached him at 8 a.m. on the 11th. Telegraphic orders were at once sent by him to the Superintendents of the corps and divisions who were to supply the men, with the result that many of them arrived the same evening, and the remainder joined by 9 a.m. the following day. In this case the men had certainly been warned some days previously that they would be wanted, but no date had been fixed. Instances of the rapid execution of orders in the other districts could be adduced, but

THE AMBULANCE BRIGADE 175

the foregoing will suffice. It speaks well for the organization of the Brigade in the districts that results such as these can be attained. Indeed, in looking back it seems as if the impossible had been achieved.

One comparison, however, may be made, which must be a source of great gratification to the Order of St. John and to every member of the Brigade. The approximate number of men in the Brigade at the end of June, 1901, was 6,500, and of these 1,313 were at that time serving in South Africa or on their way there. Thus about one in every five had then volunteered and been accepted for service.

Again, the approximate strength of the non-commissioned officers and men of the Royal Army Medical Corps who were at that time serving in or were on their way to South Africa (including Militia, Volunteers, and Brigade men) was 4,853, and of these 1,142 were Brigade men serving directly under the War Office; in other words, about one man in every four (1 in 4¼) had at that time been supplied by the Brigade. In this calculation 171 men serving in private hospitals and paid by them are not included.

Up to the 11th March, 1901, 1,934 men had been supplied by the Brigade for service in South Africa, the men serving under civil contract as members of the St. John Ambulance Brigade. On that date, however, an Army Order was issued requiring regular enlistment in the Royal Army Medical Corps, and up to the present time (1st May, 1902), only 112 Brigade men have joined that Corps as members of the Brigade, thus bringing up the total supplied for the public service to 2,046.

It is not possible to enter into any detail as to the work of the Brigade men in South Africa up to the present, and indeed until reports are rendered to the Director-General, A.M.S., on the conclusion of the war, very little information regarding the employment and services of the men can be obtained. It may be stated, however, that such unofficial reports as have come to notice from the medical officers under whom the men are serving are very satisfactory, and there is every reason to hope that, in his final report on the operations of the Army Medical Department during the war, the Director-General will be able to testify to the usefulness and good conduct of the members of the Brigade.

It speaks well for the care with which volunteers of the Brigade were selected and examined by their medical officers, that the percentage of deaths from disease in South Africa was comparatively low; but it is regretted that sixty-two men of the Brigade succumbed to disease contracted in the performance of their noble work, and it is believed that three have died in the service of the South African Constabulary. A worthy monument has been erected

THE AMBULANCE BRIGADE 177

to the memory of these gallant men in St. John's Church, a fit place for the record of their memory, for here week by week the various detachments attended their last Divine Service in England before embarkation.

The following men of the Brigade have been mentioned in despatches as having rendered special and meritorious service : Sergeants W. W. Foulkes, E. Eccles, F. H. Oldham; Privates B. B. Banks, W. Rogerson, A. England, A. Kew, and H. G. Winyard. The last-named has also been awarded the medal for Distinguished Conduct in the Field.

On the 31st May, 1902, his Majesty the King graciously presented war medals to thirty-five men of the Brigade selected from different centres in the throne room at Buckingham Palace, Prince Christian, Prince Charles of Denmark, and many members of the Chapter and Order being present.

On the afternoon of the same day a service was held in St. Paul's Cathedral which no one who was present is ever likely to forget. At the close of the service the Archdeacon of London (a chaplain), with the clergy of the Cathedral, some knights and other members of the Order, men of the Brigade and friends, proceeded to the crypt, not far from the remains of Nelson and Wellington, where the Chief Commissioner unveiled a memorial to eleven members of the District Brigade who had died in South Africa. Paying a tribute to the Commissioner of the No. 1 or London District for his work and self-devotion, he struck a chord of sympathy by saying that the men whose names were recorded had laid down their lives in really a more noble manner than those who had been killed in the heat and excitement of action. "Pro Utilitate Hominum" is inscribed at the base of the tablet, under their ever to be honoured names.

"Greater love hath no man than this, that he lay down his life for his friends," is rendered in gold letters at the base of the beautiful alabaster monument in St. John's Church, Clerkenwell, unveiled by His Royal Highness the Grand Prior on the 11th of June, 1902, of which an illustration is given. It records that it is "to the Glory of God, and in memory of those members of the St. John Ambulance Brigade who died of disease contracted while engaged in attendance on the sick and wounded during the South African Campaign, 1899-1902, erected by His Majesty King Edward VII., Sovereign Head and Patron; by His Royal Highness the Prince of Wales, K.G., Grand Prior; and by the Chapter-General of the Grand Priory of the Order of the Hospital of St. John of Jerusalem in England."

In a short address to the Grand Prior, the rector, a Chaplain of the Order, recalled that he had held services in the church for over 1,500 men before their departure for the seat of war, and of these

THE AMBULANCE BRIGADE 179

sixty-six sacrificed their lives to their duty, and also drew attention to the fact that one of the last messages of Queen Victoria was one expressing her satisfaction at the services rendered by the Brigade in South Africa.

The Dean of Gloucester in his sermon dwelt on the virtues of chivalry embodied in the knights of old, now incarnated in the modern gentleman.

H.R.H. Princess Christian was President and the Viscountess Knutsford Chairman of the St. John Ambulance Brigade War Fund for the purchase of comforts for the men on service, and she and her generous helpers earned the gratitude of the Brigade.

The Chief Commissioner, Deputy Commissioners, and their Staff Officers have rendered invaluable aid to their country and their Order.

These services have been recognized by a presentation on July 14th, 1902, at St. James's Palace, by H.R.H. the Grand Prior, of a special medal awarded for conspicuous service rendered during the South African War and with the despatch of ambulance material and medical comforts for the sick and wounded at the seat of war. The recipients were Viscount and Viscountess Knutsford, Chairman of the St. John Ambulance Association and of the Special Committee; Col. Sir Herbert Perrott, Chief Secretary of the Ambulance Department; Col. C. Bowdler, Chief Commissioner, St. John Ambulance

Brigade; Lt.-Col. C. J. Trimble, Mr. Stuart C. Wardell, Lt.-Col. G. S. Elliston, Inspector-General Belgrave Ninnis, Mr. Wm. Vernon, and Major C. H. Milburn, Deputy Commissioners, St. John Ambulance Brigade; Mr. W. J. Church-Brasier, Brigade Chief Superintendent; Lt.-Col. Richard Holbeche and Mr. W. G. Barnes, Jun., who both supervised for many months the despatch of material and medical stores for the troops; Mr. W. R. Edwards, Accountant and Storekeeper, St. John Ambulance Association; and Mr. W. H. Morgan, Chief Superintendent of the Metropolitan Corps, St. John Ambulance Brigade.

In concluding this all too desultory survey of the ancient Hospitaller work under new skies and with altered traditions, it would be wrong to omit the tribute which ought to be paid to the executive staff at St. John's Gate of every grade and degree. Foremost, however, stands the name of the Chief Secretary, Sir Herbert Perrott, Bart., whose hereditary connection with the revived Order of St. John has throughout his long period of office induced him to promote its interests with able and unflagging devotion. Whatever scheme for the widening of its area of usefulness has been evolved, it has invariably found in him a strenuous supporter and an ever vigilant guardian of the interests of the Order.

APPENDIX A

RECEPTION OF A KNIGHT

(From Woodhouse, "Military Religious Orders," 1879)

THE postulant presented himself with a lighted taper in his hand, and carrying his naked sword. After blessing the sword, the priest returned it to him with these words: "Receive this sword in the name of the Father and of the Son and of the Holy Ghost, Amen, and use it for thine own defence and that of the Church of God, to the confusion of the enemies of Jesus Christ and of the Christian faith, and take heed that no human frailty move thee to strike any man with it unjustly." Then he replaced it in the sheath, the priest saying, as the knight girded himself, "Gird thyself with the sword of Jesus Christ, and remember that it is not with the sword but with faith that the saints have conquered kingdoms."

The knight then once more drew his sword, and these words were addressed to him: "Let the brilliancy of this sword represent to thee the brightness of faith, let its point signify hope, and its hilt charity. Use it for the Catholic faith, for justice, and for the consolation of widows and orphans, for this is the true faith and justification of a Christian knight." Then he brandished it thrice in the name of the Holy Trinity.

The brethren then proceeded to give him his golden spurs, saying, "Seest thou these spurs? They signify that as the horse fears them when he swerves from his duty, so shouldest thou fear to depart from thy post or from thy vows."

Then the mantle was thrown over him, and they pointed to the cross of eight points embroidered on the left side, and said: "We wear this white cross as a sign of purity; wear it also within thy heart as well as outwardly, and keep it without soil or stain. The eight points are the signs of the eight beatitudes which thou must ever preserve, viz., 1. Spiritual joy; 2. To live without malice; 3. To weep over thy sins; 4. To humble thyself to those who injure thee; 5. To love justice; 6. To be merciful; 7. To be sincere and pure of heart; 8. To suffer persecution."

Then he kissed the cross, and the mantle was fastened, whilst the ministering knight continued: "Take this cross and mantle in the name of the Holy Trinity for the repose and salvation of thy soul, the defence of the Catholic faith and the honour of our Lord Jesus Christ. I place it on thy left side near thy heart that thou mayest love it, and that thy right hand may defend it, charging thee never to abandon it, since it is the standard of our holy faith. Shouldest thou ever desert thy standard, and fly when combating the enemies of Jesus Christ, thou wilt be stripped of this holy sign, according to the statutes of the Order, as having broken the vow thou hast taken, and shalt be cut off from our body as an unsound member."

On the mantle were embroidered all the instruments of the Passion; each of them was pointed out to the new-made knight, with the words: "In order that thou mayest put all thy hope in the Passion of Jesus Christ, behold the cord whereby He was bound; see, too, His crown of thorns; this is the column to which He was tied; this is the lance which pierced His side; this is the sponge with which He was drenched with vinegar and gall; these are the whips that scourged Him; this is the Cross on which He suffered. Receive therefore the yoke of the Lord, for it is easy and light, and will give rest unto thy soul; and I tie this cord about thy neck in pledge of the servitude thou hast promised. We offer thee nothing but bread and water, and a simple habit and of little worth. We give thee and thy parents and relations a share in the good works performed by the Order, and by our brethren now and hereafter throughout the world. Amen."

He was then received with the kiss of peace.

APPENDIX B

COMMANDERIES OF THE ORDER OF ST. JOHN IN ENGLAND

(From Porter)

COUNTY.	COMMANDERY.	INCOME.		
Berkshire,	Grenham, including Shaldeford.	£76	13	6
Wiltshire,	Anesty	93	0	0
Dorsetshire,	Mayne, including Kyngeston and Waye	96	2	10
Cornwall,	Trebyghen	75	11	4
Devonshire,	Bothemescomb, including Coue	50	11	0
Somersetshire,	Bucklands, including Halse .	124	10	4
Hampshire,	Godesfield, including Badeslee and Runham . . .	66	13	11
Sussex,	Palyng	78	11	3
Oxford,	Clanefeld	60	13	4
Gloucestershire,	Quenyngton	179	8	4
Herefordshire,	Dynemoor, including Sutton, Rolston, and Wormbrigge .	182	7	3
Pembrokeshire,	Slebech	307	1	10
North Wales,	Halstan, including Dongewal .	157	5	10
Warwickshire,	Grafton	78	15	2
Derbyshire,	Yeveley	95	6	0
Yorkshire,	Newland	56	5	4
,,	Mount St. John . . .	58	8	4
,,	Beverley	83	17	6
Northumberland,	Chibourn	23	18	8
Nottinghamshire,	Oscington	95	0	8
Lincolnshire,	Maltby	116	6	8
,,	Skirbeck	84	11	8

COUNTY.	COMMANDERY.	INCOME.
Leicestershire,	Dalby, including Beaumont	128 15 8
Northamptonshire,	Dyngley	79 4 0
Buckinghamshire,	Hoggeshawe	74 14 10
Bedfordshire,	Melcheburn	106 2 4
,,	Hardwyck, including Clifton and Pelyng	69 3 5
Cambridgeshire,	Shenegeye, including Wendeye, Arnyngton, and Cranden	187 12 8
,,	Chippenham	110 16 9
Norfolk,	Kerbrok	192 2 4
Suffolk,	Batesford, including Codenham and Melles	93 10 8
Essex,	Maplestrestede	77 16 8
,,	Staundon	34 15 4
Kent,	Swenefeld	82 4 4
,,	Sutton atte Hone	40 0 0
Middlesex,	Clerkenwell	400 0 0

Woodhouse adds to these: Brompton in Berkshire; Temple Rockley, Wiltshire; Temple Combe in Somerset; Temple Cowley (or Sandford) and Gosford in Oxfordshire; Warwick and Temple Balsall in Warwickshire; Waingeif in Derbyshire; Ribstone in Yorkshire: Temple Brewer, Eagle, Wilketon, Mere, Witham, and Aslackby in Lincolnshire; Heather, Temple Rothley, and Swinford in Leicestershire; Great Wilbraham in Cambridgeshire; Holstone, or Hawston, in Norfolk; Gislingham in Suffolk; Temple Cressing in Essex; Peckham in Kent; Hampton in Middlesex; Barrow in Cheshire; Temple Dynnesley and Standon in Hertfordshire; Dingley in Northamptonshire. Several of these were Preceptories of the Knights Templars.

APPENDIX C

GRAND PRIORS OF ENGLAND

(FROM PORTER)

THE account of the Grand Priors previous to the commencement of the fourteenth century is very incomplete and unsatisfactory. Very probably the names of many of the Conventual Priors of St. John of Clerkenwell are mixed up with them. The following list is given as they occur in the Cott. MSS., as far as the name of William de Tottenham. From him to the conclusion of the roll the vouchers are to be found in the " Libri Bullarum," in the Record Office, at Malta.

1. GARNIER DE NEAPOLIS. Is the first recorded Grand Prior of England. He could not have been the Garnier de Neapolis, afterwards Grand Master, who died of wounds received at the battle of Tiberias, A.D. 1187. An ancient MS. quoted by Paolo Antonio Paoli, in the possession of the Canon Smitmer, of Vienna, proves that he was living, and Prior of England, A.D. 1189. He was in all probability a brother of the Grand Master.
2. RICHARD DE TURK. Was living in the time of the first Prioress of Buckland.
3. RALPH DE DYNHAM, or DINANT.
4. GILBERT DE VERE. He bestowed on the Dames of Buckland a pension of a hundred crowns charged upon his manor of Rainham.
5. HUGH D'ALNETO, or DANET.
6. ALAN. Afterwards Bishop of Bangor, was probably only Conventual Prior of Clerkenwell.
7. ROBERT THE TREASURER.

186 HOSPITALLERS OF ST. JOHN

8. THEODORIC DE NUSSA, *or* NYSSA. "There went from the Hospitaller's House of Clerkenwell, in London, a great number of Knights, with banner displayed, preceded by Brother Theodoric, their Prior, a German by nation, who set out for Palestine with a considerable body of troops in their pay. These Knights, passing over London Bridge, saluted with their capuce in hand all the inhabitants that crowded to see them pass, and recommended themselves to their prayers." Matth. Paris, *sub ann.* 1237, p. 444.
9. ROBERT DE MAUNEBY, Prior.
10. ROBERT DE VERE. Was witness, as Conservator of the Hospital, in a Charter, dated Acre, 19th December, 1262. He gave to the Church of Clerkenwell, in 1269, one of the six water-pots in which the water was changed into wine at the marriage of Cana in Galilee. As Prior he visited the Convent of Buckland, to arrange some disputes, and died 15th February, 1270.
11. PETER DE HOCKHAM. Named in a bull of Pope Boniface VIII., A.D. 1295.
12. SIMON BOCARD.
13. ELIAS SINGLETON, *or* SMELHTON.
14. STEPHEN FULBURN.
15. JOSEPH DE CHAUNCY. He built the chapel of the Lord Prior, in the Conventual House of Clerkenwell; *temp.* Edward I.
16. WALTER. Gained possession of the Preceptories of Quenyngton-Schenegaye, and other lands and tenements.
17. WILLIAM DE HENLEY. Built the cloisters of the House of Clerkenwell, A.D. 1283-4, and *ob.* 4th February the same year.
18. RICHARD DE PENLEY. Was Prior before 1307.
19. ROBERT DE DYNHAM, *or* DINANT.
20. WILLIAM DE TOTTENHAM. The name of this Grand Prior is written both *Cochal* and *Tothal,* but his real name as here given is proved by a letter from the Archbishop of Canterbury, Walter Rainold, to William de Tottenham, Grand Prior of the Knights Hospitallers of Jerusalem, dated Lambeth, 17th July, 1314. *Vide* Rymer and Du Puy, "Hist. des Templiers," 4to, 1751, p. 478. He died 12th October, 1318.
21. THOMAS L'ARCHER. Was removed from the office of Prior

APPENDIX C

at the request of King Edward II., being incapacitated to fulfil the duties from age and infirmities, A.D. 1329.

22. LEONARD DE TIBERTIS. Named by some authorities *De Theobaldi*, being Prior of Venice. Was nominated by the Grand Master, De Villeneuve, Visitor of the English Priory, and afterwards appointed Grand Prior of England, at the special request of King Edward II., A.D. 1329-30.

23. PHILIP DE TAME. Was Prior of England, A.D. 1335, 10th Edward III., and died before A.D. 1358.

JOHN DE DALTON. Is said by Paoli to have been called Prior of England in a bull of the Grand Master, Berenger, but as his name does not appear as such in any of the "Libri Bullarum," he was probably only Prior of the Conventual Church of Clerkenwell.

24. JOHN DE PAVELEY. Lieutenant Prior and Turcopolier, named Grand Prior of England in a bull of the Grand Master, Roger de Pins, dated Rhodes, 14th October, 1358. *Ob.* 1371.

25. ROBERT DE HALES. Preceptor of Slebiche and Saundford; Bailli of Aquila. Nominated Grand Prior of England *vice* Paveley, A.D. 1371. Beheaded on Tower Hill, A.D. 1381.

26. JOHN DE REDINGTON. Preceptor of Ribestone, Bailli of Aquila. Nominated Grand Prior of England on the death of Robert de Hales, by bull of the Grand Master, John de Heredia, dated Rhodes, 18th November, 1381. *Ob.* 1399.

27. WALTER DE GRENDON. Preceptor of Halstone. Named Prior of England by bull of the Grand Master, Philibert de Naillac, dated Rhodes, 18th October, 1400. *Ob.* 1416.

28. WILLIAM HULLES. Preceptor of Swynefield, Templecombe, and Quenyngton. Nominated Grand Prior of England by bull of the Grand Master, Philibert de Naillac, dated Rhodes, 16th July, 1417. *Ob.* A.D. 1433.

29. ROBERT MALLORY. Preceptor of Greneham, Balsal, and Grafton. Elected Grand Prior of England by bull of the Grand Master, Anthony Fluvian, dated Rhodes, 4th May, 1433. *Ob.* A.D. 1440.

30. ROBERT BOUTIL, *or* BOTYLL. Preceptor of Melchebourne, Anstey, and Trebighe. Made Grand Prior of England by bull

of the Grand Master, Jean de Lastic, dated Rhodes, 29th November, 1440. *Ob.* A.D. 1468.[1]

31. JOHN LANGSTROTHER. Preceptor of Balsal and Grafton; Lieutenant Turcopolier; Receiver-General of England; Castellan of Rhodes; Bailli of Aquila; Seneschal of the Grand Master; Commander of Cyprus. Nominated Grand Prior of England by bull of the Grand Master, Jean Baptiste Orsini, dated Rhodes, 5th April, 1470. Made prisoner, and beheaded after the battle of Tewkesbury, by order of Edward IV., A.D. 1741. Buried in the Church of St. John, at Clerkenwell.

32. WILLIAM TORNAY. Preceptor of Baddesley and Mayne; Receiver-General of England; Bailli of Aquila. Appointed Grand Prior of England by bull of the Grand Master, John Baptiste Orsini, dated Rhodes, 29th August, 1471. *Ob.* A.D. 1476.

33. JOHN WESTON. Preceptor of Newland and Dynemore; Lieut. Turcopolier; Turcopolier. Appointed Grand Prior of England by bull of the Grand Master, Pierre d'Aubusson, dated Rhodes, 24th July, 1476. *Ob.* A.D. 1489.

34. JOHN KENDAL. Preceptor of Willoughton, Halstone, and Ribestone; Turcopolier. Nominated Grand Prior of England by bull of the Grand Master, Pierre d'Aubusson, dated Rhodes, 20th June, 1489. *Ob.* A.D. 1501.

35. THOMAS DOCWRA. Preceptor of Dynemore; Lieutenant Turcopolier; Prior of Ireland; Turcopolier. Elected Grand Prior of England by bull of the Grand Master, Pierre d'Aubusson, dated Rhodes, 6th August, 1501. *Ob.* A.D. 1527.

36. WILLIAM WESTON. Preceptor of Baddesley and Mayne; Turcopolier. Named Grand Prior of England by bull of the Grand Master, Philip Villiers de L'Isle Adam, dated Corneto, 27th June, 1527. Died of grief for the dissolution of the Language of England, A.D. 1540. Buried in the Church of St. John at Clerkenwell.

37. THOMAS TRESHAM. Appointed Grand Prior of England by a Royal Charter of Queen Mary, dated Greenwich, 2nd April, 1557.

---

[1] Arms in east window of St. John's Church, Clerkenwell.

APPENDIX C 189

38. RICHARD SHELLEY. Turcopolier, 2nd April, 1557. Named Grand Prior of England on the death of Thomas Tresham, A.D. 1566; supposed to have died at Venice, *circa* 1589-90.
39. ANDREW WYSE. Bailli of Aquila, 1588. Nominated Grand Prior of England by papal brief, A.D. 1593. *Ob.* A.D. 1631.
40. HENRY FITZ-JAMES. Natural son of King James II. of England. Nominated Grand Prior of England on visiting Malta, by bull of the Grand Master, Gregorio Caraffa, A.D. 1687; quitted the habit of the Order, and resigned the Grand Priory, A.D. 1701.

TITULAR GRAND PRIORS OF ENGLAND

41. FRANÇOIS ASTORG DE SEGREVILLE. Nominated Grand Prior of England by his uncle, the Grand Master, Loubens de Verdale, by bull, dated Malta, 22nd April, 1591, but obliged to resign the dignity on protest to the Pope of the Bailli of Aquila, Andrew Wyse; created instead Bailli of Aquila, 8th June, 1593.
42. CESARE FERETTI. Assisted at a Chapter-General, A.D. 1612, as Prior of England, Andrew Wyse still living.
43. GIOVANNI BATTISTA NARI. Elected Grand Prior of England by papal brief, A.D. 1631.
44. ALESSANDRO ZAMBECCARI. Nominated by papal brief, dated Rome, 9th May, 1639, Grand Prior of England.
45. GERONIMO ALLIATA. Elected Grand Prior of England by papal brief, dated Rome, 5th June, 1648.
46. STEFANO MARIA LOMELLINO. Named by papal brief Grand Prior of England, dated Rome, 19th June, 1654.
47. GIULIO BOVIO. Commander of San Giovanni di Tortona and Orvieto. Appointed Grand Prior of England by brief of Pope Clement XI., dated Rome, 11th July, 1701. *Ob.* A.D. 1706.
48. FRANCESCO MARIA FERRETTI. Nominated Grand Prior of England by brief of Pope Clement XI., dated Rome, 11th December, 1706; registered in Council, 26th March, 1707. Resigned the Grand Priory.

49. NICOLO GIRALDIN. Appointed Grand Prior of England by papal brief, dated Rome, 9th August, 1726; registered in Council, 18th August, 1732.
50. PETER FITZ-JAMES. Nominated Grand Prior of England by papal brief. No date given.
51. BUONAVENTURA FITZ-JAMES. Grand Prior of England, named by papal brief; registered in Council, 13th May, A.D. 1734; resigned the dignity and the habit, A.D. 1755.
52. GIOVANNI BATTISTA ALTIERI. Appointed Grand Prior of England by brief of Pope Benedict XIV., dated Rome, 20th September, 1755; registered in Council, 23rd October, 1755. Resigned the dignity, being appointed Grand Prior of Venice.
53. GIROLAMO LAPARELLI. Grand Prior of England, living at Catania, A.D. 1806.

TURCOPOLIERS OF THE ENGLISH LANGUAGE

The Turcopolier was the title peculiar to the head of the venerable Language of England: he was commander of the Turcopoles or Light Cavalry, and had also the care of the coast defences of the two islands of Rhodes and Malta. Upon the death of the Turcopolier Nicholas Upton, A.D. 1551, it was determined by the Council that no more Turcopoliers should be elected till the religious troubles in England should be satisfactorily arranged; which decree was confirmed by papal briefs and the office of Turcopoliers at the same time incorporated with the dignity of Grand Master, in the years 1583, 1584, and 1613.

1. PETER DE SARDINES. Turcoplerius: was witness to a Charter of the Abbot of St. Mary of the Latins, in Jerusalem, granting the casal of Montdisder to the Knights Hospitallers of St. John of Jerusalem, A.D. 1248.
2. JOHN DE BUISBROX, *or* BRAYBROOK. Was nominated Turcopolier at a General Chapter, held at Montpelier, on the 24th October, 1329-30, under the Grand Master, Elion de Villeneuve, when the grand dignities were attached to the

eight Languages, that of Turcopolier being confirmed to England.
3. JOHN DE PAVELEY. Named Turcopolier in a bull, dated A.D. 1335, Grand Prior.
4. WILLIAM DE MIDLETON. Preceptor of Ribestone and Mount St. John. Named Turcopolier in a bull of the Grand Master, Raymond Berenger, dated Rhodes, 28th January, 1365-6.
5. RICHARD DE OVERTONE. Preceptor of Mount St. John, Receiver of England; named Turcopolier in a brief of Pope Gregory XI., dated Avignon, December, A.D. 1375.
6. BRIAN DE GREY. Named Turcopolier in a bull of the Grand Master, John de Heredia, dated Rhodes, 22nd February, 1385-6, confirming to him the Bailliage of Aquila for life, and the Preceptory of Beverley, *in commendam*. *Ob.* 1389.
7. HILDEBRAND INGE. Preceptor of Buckland, and Receiver-General of England. Nominated Turcopolier in a bull of the Grand Master, John de Heredia, dated Rhodes, 20th October, 1392.
8. PETER DE HOLTE. Prior of Ireland. Appointed Turcopolier in a bull of the Grand Master, Philibert de Naillac, confirming to him also the Priory of Ireland for ten years, dated Rhodes, 2nd August, 1396. *Ob.* A.D. 1415.
9. THOMAS DE SKIPWITH. Preceptor of Beverley and Schenegaye: named Turcopolier in a bull of the Grand Master, Philibert de Naillac, dated Rhodes, 10th September, 1417. He resigns the Turcopoliership on being appointed Commander of Cyprus, 1421. *Ob.* A.D. 1422.
10. THOMAS LAUNCELYN. Preceptor of Baddesley, Dalby, and Rotheley. Appointed Turcopolier, on resignation of Thomas de Skipwith, by bull of the Grand Master, Anthony Fluvian, dated Rhodes, 3rd October, 1421. *Ob.* A.D. 1442.
11. HUGH MIDLETON. Preceptor of Willoughton and Beverley, Bailli of Aquila: made Turcopolier by bull of the Grand Master, Jean de Lastic, dated Rhodes, 19th June, 1422. *Ob.* A.D. 1449.
12. WILLIAM DAUNAY. Preceptor of Dynemore. Elected Turcopolier, on the death of Hugh Midleton, by bull of the Grand

Master, Jean de Lastic, dated Rhodes, 18th June, 1449. *Ob.* 1468.

13. ROBERT TONG. Preceptor of Mount St. John. Named Turcopolier by bull of the Grand Master, John Baptist Orsini, dated Rhodes, A.D. 1468; resigned the Turcopoliership on being nominated Bailli of Aquila, A.D. 1471.

14. JOHN WESTON. Preceptor of Newland and Dynemore. Appointed Turcopolier, on mutition of Robert Tong, by bull of the Grand Master, John Baptist Orsini, dated Rhodes, 16th October, A.D. 1471; afterwards Grand Prior of England.

15. JOHN KENDAL. Preceptor of Willoughton. Elected Turcopolier by bull of the Grand Master, Pierre d'Aubusson, dated Rhodes, 14th March, 1476-7, on the elevation of John Weston to be Grand Prior; and whom he also succeeded in that dignity, 1489.

16. JOHN BOSVILE. Preceptor of Temple-Bruer and Quenyngton; nominated Turcopolier by bull of the Grand Master, Pierre d'Aubusson, Rhodes, 20th June, A.D. 1489. *Ob.* A.D. 1494.

17. THOMAS DOCWRA. Preceptor of Dynemore, Prior of Ireland; named Turcopolier in a brief, dated Rhodes, 14th October, 1495; succeeded to the Grand Priory of England, A.D. 1501.

18. THOMAS NEWPORT. Preceptor of Newland and Temple-Bruer; Receiver of the Common Treasury; made Turcopolier, *vice* Docwra; nominated Grand Prior, A.D. 1501; Bailli of Aquila by mutition, 1502.

19. ROBERT DANIEL. Preceptor of Swinefield; nominated Turcopolier by brief of the Grand Master, Cardinal Pierre d'Aubusson, dated Rhodes, 30th March, 1502-3.

20. WILLIAM DARELL. Preceptor of Willoughton, Lieutenant Turcopolier; named Turcopolier in a bull of Emeri d'Amboise, Grand Master, dated Rhodes, 5th February, 1509-10. *Ob.* A.D. 1519.

21. JOHN BOOTH, BOUCH, *or* BUCK. Preceptor of Quenyngton, Anstey, and Trebigh; Receiver-General; named Turcopolier in succession to William Darell, A.D. 1519; was slain at the third and most desperate assault on the bulwark of England, at the siege of Rhodes, A.D. 1522.

APPENDIX C 193

22. WILLIAM WESTON. Preceptor of Baddesley and Mayne, etc.; elected Turcopolier in the Chapter held in Candia, after the expulsion of the Order from Rhodes, 1523; commanded the grand carracque of the Order; made Grand Prior, A.D. 1527.
23. JOHN RAWSON. Preceptor of Swinefield; Prior of Ireland; nominated Turcopolier by bull of Philip Villiers de L'Isle Adam, Grand Master, dated Corneto, 27th June, 1527. Was reappointed Prior of Ireland, resigning the dignity of Turcopolier.
24. JOHN BABINGTON. Preceptor of Dalby and Rotheley; Prior of Ireland; Receiver-General. Elected Turcopolier by bull of the Grand Master, L'Isle Adam, dated "from our Priory House of the Hospital in England," 4th June, 1528. Bailli of Aquila by mutition, 1530-1.
25. CLEMENT WEST (deprived). Preceptor of Slebeche; Receiver of the Common Treasury; named Turcopolier by bull of L'Isle Adam, Grand Master, dated Malta, 7th January, 1530-1. Deprived of the habit and dignity for insubordinate conduct, A.D. 1533.
26. ROGER BOYDEL. Preceptor of Halstone, Baddesley, and Mayne; appointed Turcopolier, *vice* Clement West, deprived February, A.D. 1533. *Ob.* March, 1533.
27. JOHN RAWSON, Jun. Preceptor of Quenyngton; Receiver of the Treasury; nominated Turcopolier by bull of the Grand Master, L'Isle Adam, dated Malta, 19th April, 1533. Resigned that dignity, and elected instead Bailli of Aquila, 1534-5.

CLEMENT WEST (restored). Was restored to the habit and the dignity of Turcopolier, 15th February, 1534-5; and again deprived and imprisoned, A.D. 1539. *Ob.* A.D. 1547.
28. GYLES RUSSEL. Preceptor of Baddesfort and Dingley; Lieutenant Turcopolier; Captain of Il Borgho; nominated Turcopolier, *vice* West, deprived A.D. 1539. *Ob.* A.D. 1543.

(OSWALD MASSINGBERD, Lieutenant Turcopolier.) Lieutenant Turcopolier, so named, *vice* Russel, dead; nominated Prior of Ireland under certain conditions, A.D. 1547.
29. NICHOLAS UPTON. Preceptor of Ribestone. Elected Turcopolier by bull of the Grand Master, John d'Omedes, dated

Malta, 5th November, 1548. Died of a *coup-de-soleil*, received whilst repelling a landing of the Turks on the Island of Malta, A.D. 1551.

(OSWALD MASSINGBERD, again.) Lieutenant Turcopolier, so nominated again on the death of the Turcopolier Upton. Confirmed Prior of Ireland, A.D. 1555.

30. RICHARD SHELLEY. Preceptor of Slebeche and Halstone: nominated Turcopolier by charter of Mary, Queen of England, dated Greenwich, 2nd April, 1557; afterwards Grand Prior, 1566.

TITULAR TURCOPOLIERS

DON PEDRO GONSALEZ DE MENDOZA. Son of the Viceroy of Naples; named Turcopolier by papal brief, A.D. 1576; resigns the dignity, 1578; nominated Prior of Ireland, A.D. 1582.

FRANÇOIS DE L'ESPINAY-ST. LUC. Appointed Turcopolier by brief of Pope Pius V., while yet in his novitiate. On protest from the whole Order, the obnoxious appointment was revoked, A.D. 1606.

JOHANN BAPTIST VON FLACKSLANDEN. Bailli of the Anglo-Bavarian Language; elected Turcopolier, registered in Council, 7th November, 1782, Emmanuel de Rohan, Grand Master; Bailli of Aquila by mutition, 1794-5.

BAILLIS OF AQUILA, OR OF THE EAGLE

The Bailliage of Ecle, Eycle, Egle, Eagle or Aquila, a preceptory situated about seven miles from the city of Lincoln, was granted to the Knights Templars by King Stephen, about 1139. At the suppression of that Order it passed into possession of the Knights Hospitallers of St. John of Jerusalem.

1. ROBERT CORT. The first named Preceptor of the Eycle in the report of the possessions of the Knights Hospitallers, made by the Grand Prior of England, Philip de Thame, to the Grand Master, Elion de Villeneuve, A.D. 1338.

2. JOHN DE ANLABY. Called Preceptor of Eycle, in a grant to

APPENDIX C

him of certain Commanderies by the Grand Master, Dieudonné de Gozon. Bull dated Rhodes, 1st August, 1351.

3. ROBERT DE HALES. Preceptor of Beverley and the Ecle; so called in a bull of the Grand Master, Roger de Pins, dated Rhodes, 1st June, 1358; afterwards Grand Prior of England.
4. JOHN DE DINGLEY. Preceptor of Dalby and the Ycle; named in a bull of Raymond Berenger, Grand Master, dated Rhodes, 20th February, 1365-6.
5. JOHN DE MANEBY. Preceptor of the Eagle. Named in a grant of the Grand Master, D'Heredia, dated Rhodes, 18th November, 1381, as having died that year.
6. JOHN DE REDINGTON. Received the Bailliage of the Eagle, to hold as a "fifth Commandery," being at this time Grand Prior of England, by grant of the same Grand Master. Bull, dated Rhodes, 18th November, 1381.
7. BRIAN DE GREY. Preceptor of Beverley; Turcopolier receives for life a grant of the Bailliage of Aquila, resigned by the Grand Prior, Redington. Bull, dated February, 1385-6. Heredia, Grand Master. To hold with the office of Turcopolier.
8. HENRY CROWNAL. Preceptor of Willoughton; succeeded to the Bailliage of Aquila on the death of Brian de Grey, September, 1389. *Ob.* A.D. 1433.
9. WILLIAM POOLE. Preceptor of Dynemore and Garrewayes; nominated Bailli of Aquila by bull of the Grand Master, Anthony Fluvian, dated Rhodes, 19th July, 1433; resigned the dignity, 1438, and died the same year.
10. HUGH MIDLETON. Preceptor of Beverley; made Bailli of Aquila by bull of the Grand Master, De Lastic, dated Rhodes, 23rd January, 1438-9; Turcopolier by mutition, 1442. *Ob.* 1449.
11. WILLIAM LANGSTROTHER. Preceptor of Quenyngton; appointed Bailli of Aquila by bull dated Rhodes, 19th June, 1442; John de Lastic, Grand Master. *Ob.* A.D. 1463.
12. JOHN LANGSTROTHER. Preceptor of Beverley, Balsal, Ribestone, etc.; Lieutenant Turcopolier, etc. Created Bailli of Aquila by bull of the Grand Master, De Lastic, dated Rhodes, 28th February, 1463-4; promoted to be Grand Prior of England, A.D. 1470; beheaded, 1471.

196 HOSPITALLERS OF ST. JOHN

13. WILLIAM TORNAY. Preceptor of Dalby and Rotheley; Receiver-General. Nominated Bailli of Aquila, bull dated Rhodes, 5th April, 1470; John Baptist Orsini, Grand Master. Grand Prior of England, 1471. *Ob.* 1476.
14. ROBERT TONG. Preceptor of Mount St. John; Turcopolier; mutitioned Bailli of Aquila by bull of the Grand Master, Orsini, dated Rhodes, 29th August, 1471. *Ob.* A.D. 1481.
15. THOMAS GREEN. Preceptor of Schenegaye. Nominated Bailli of Aquila by bull of the Grand Master, Pierre d'Aubusson, dated Rhodes, 11th July, 1481. *Ob.* A.D. 1502.
16. THOMAS NEWPORT. Preceptor of Newland, etc.; Receiver-General of England; Turcopolier. Transferred to the Bailliage of Aquila by mutition, bull dated Rhodes, 10th March, 1502-3; D'Aubusson, Grand Master. Drowned on the coast of Spain, hastening to the relief of Rhodes, besieged by the Turks, A.D. 1522.
17. THOMAS SHEFFIELD. Preceptor of Beverley; Receiver-General of England; Seneschal of the Grand Master. Named Bailli of Aquila by bull of the Grand Master, L'Isle Adam, dated Messina, 4th May, 1523. *Ob.* at Viterbo, A.D. 1524.
18. ALBAN POLE. Preceptor of Newland, Ossington, and Winklebourne. Appointed Bailli of Aquila by bull of the Grand Master, L'Isle Adam, dated Viterbo, 26th August, 1524. *Ob.* A.D. 1530.
19. JOHN BABINGTON. Preceptor of Dalby, etc.; Prior of Ireland; Receiver-General of England; Turcopolier. Made Bailli of Aquila by mutition, bull dated Malta, 7th January, 1530-1. *Ob.* A.D. 1533-4.
20. JOHN RAWSON, Jun. Preceptor of Quenyngton; Receiver-General; Turcopolier. Bailli of Aquila, bull dated Malta, 15th February, 1534-5; Pierre de Ponte, Grand Master.
21. PEDRO FELICES DE LA NUCA. Commander of the Language of Aragon: created Bailli of Aquila by charter of Mary, Queen of England, dated Greenwich, 2nd April, 1557. Was slain at the siege of Malta, A.D. 1565.
22. OLIVER STARKEY. Commander of Quenyngton; Lieutenant Turcopolier; Bailli of Aquila by bull of the Grand Master,

APPENDIX C 197

Pierre de Monte, Malta, 3rd October, 1569. *Ob.* 1588. Buried in the vault of the Grand Masters in the Conventual Church of St. John, the only Knight of the Order so distinguished.

23. ANDREW WYSE. Nominated Bailli of Aquila on death of Oliver Starkey, being the only English Knight in the Convent, Malta, 27th April, 1588; Loubens de Verdala, Grand Master; was afterwards Grand Prior of England, 1593. *Ob.* A.D. 1631.

TITULAR BAILLIS OF AQUILA

24. FRANÇOIS D'ASTORG DE SEGREVILLE. Appointed Bailli of Aquila by bull of the Grand Master, Verdale, dated Malta, 8th June, 1593. *Ob.* A.D. 1612.
25. LUIS MENDEZ DE VASCONCELLOS. A Portuguese Commander of the Language of Castile: named Bailli of Aquila by bull of the Grand Master, Alof de Vignacourt, Malta, 29th August, 1612; afterwards Grand Master.
26. MICHEL DE PONTAILLER-THALLEMEY. Nominated Bailli of Aquila by brief, dated Malta, 20th February, 1622. *Ob.* A.D. 1630.
27. JEAN DE BERNOIS-VILLENEUVE. Appointed Bailli of Aquila, on the death of Thallemey, 13th June, 1630. *Ob.* A.D. 1656.
28. OTTAVIO BANDINELLI. Named Bailli of Aquila by papal brief, Rome, 22nd April, 1656.
29. JACQUES DE SPARVIER-CORBONNEAU. Nominated Bailli of Aquila by brief, 14th May, 1671; Grand Commander, 1672.
30. DON DIEGO BRAGAMONTE. Made Bailli of Aquila by brief of Pope Clement X., 22nd May, 1673. *Ob.* A.D. 1690.
31. DON EMANUEL DE TORDESILLAS. Created Bailli of Aquila by papal brief of Alexander VIII., 20th September, 1690. *Ob.* A.D. 1702.
32. RICHARD DE SADE-MAZAN. Commander of Puysmaison: named Bailli of Aquila by brief of Pope Clement XI., 18th August, 1702; registered in Council, 11th September, 1702; Grand Commander, 1714.
33. ANTONIO DOMENICO BUSSI. Commander: appointed Bailli of

Aquila by brief of Pope Clement XI., dated Rome, 23rd June, 1714; registered in Council, 28th July, 1715.

34. FRANCESCO DE GUEDEZ-PEREIRA. A Commander of Portugal; Vice-Chancellor: nominated Bailli of Aquila by papal brief, dated Rome, 22nd March, 1755.
35. HENRI FRANÇOIS DE GUIRAN LA BRILLANE. Elected Bailli of Aquila by papal brief of Pius VI., Rome, 18th May, 1781; registered in Council, 12th July, 1781.
36. NORBERT VON TORRING. Commander of Erding, of the Anglo-Bavarian Language; named Bailli of Aquila by brief of Pope Pius VI.; registered in Council, 10th September, 1790; afterwards Lieutenant Turcopolier, 1792.
37. JOHANN BAPTISTE VON FLACHSLANDEN. Turcopolier (Titular) of the Anglo-Bavarian Language; nominated Bailli of Aquila by brief of Pope Pius VI.; registered in Council, 26th February, 1794-5.

PRIORS OF IRELAND

No mention occurs of a Prior of Ireland before the Chapter-General of the Order held at Montpellier, A.D. 1329-30, Elion de Villeneuve, Grand Master.

1. ROGER WEILLAM. Was present as "Prior Hibernia prioratûs" at the General Chapter held at Montpellier, Elion de Villeneuve, Grand Master, presiding, A.D. 1329-30.
2. JOHN L'ARCHER. Preceptor of Dalby and Mayne; Prior of Ireland; named in a bull of the Grand Master, Dieudonné de Gozon, dated Rhodes, 28th October, 1351.
3. THOMAS DE BURLE. Preceptor of Dynemore and Barrowe; named Prior of Ireland in a bull dated Rhodes, 15th February, 1365; Raymond Berenger, Grand Master.
4. WILLIAM DE TABNEY. Named Prior of Ireland in a bull of the Grand Master, D'Heredia, dated Rhodes, 24th March, 1381-2; was present as Prior of Ireland at a General Council, 2nd August, 1382.
5. PETER DE HOLTE. Was Prior of Ireland previous to 1396. On being nominated Turcopolier by bull of the Grand Master,

APPENDIX C

Philibert de Naillac, dated Rhodes, the 2nd August of that year, he was therein confirmed Prior of Ireland for ten years longer. Resigned the Priory of Ireland, 1410, and died A.D. 1415.

6. THOMAS LE BOUTELER. Named Prior of Ireland in a bull of the Lieutenancy of the Grand Master, De Naillac, Rhodes, 12th May, 1410. *Ob.* A.D. 1420.
7. RICHARD PAULE. Preceptor of Temple-Bruer; nominated Prior of Ireland by bull of the Grand Master, De Naillac, dated Rhodes, 31st October, 1420. Resigned the Priory of Ireland, 1422.
8. WILLIAM FITZ-THOMAS. Appointed Prior of Ireland by a bull of the Grand Master, Fluvian, dated Rhodes, 24th June, 1422.

   (MAURICE FITZ-WILLIAM.) The Priory of Ireland was seized upon and wrongfully usurped, without any nomination of the Grand Master and Council, on the death of William Fitz-Thomas, the Prior, by Maurice Fitz-William. He being shortly after deprived by the unanimous act of the Irish Knights, the nomination of a successor was left in the hands of the Grand Master and Council, A.D. 1440.
9. EDMOND ASHETON. Preceptor of Anstey and Trebigh; was nominated to the vacant Priory of Ireland by the Grand Master, Jean de Lastic; bull, dated Rhodes, 12th July, 1440. *Ob.* A.D. 1442.
10. HUGH MIDLETON. Preceptor of Willoughton and Beverley; Bailli of Aquila; Turcopolier; nominated Visitor of the Priory of Ireland by bull dated Rhodes, 20th November, 1442; afterwards confirmed Prior, as appears by a bull of the Grand Master, De Lastic, dated Rhodes, 12th September, 1450.

    (THOMAS TALBOT.) Was nominated Administrator of the Priory of Ireland, 1446-9. Owing to his maladministration, and letters written from the King, Henry VI., from the Council of the Irish Commanders, and from the Chapter of the Priory of Dublin, he was removed from his office.
11. THOMAS FITZ-GERALD. Confirmed Prior of Ireland, at the request of the Irish Commanders, by bull of the Grand Master, De Lastic, dated Rhodes, 10th September, 1450. *Ob.* A.D. 1453.

12. THOMAS TALBOT. Appointed Prior of Ireland, notwithstanding his former deprivation, on the death of Fitz-Gerald, by bull dated Rhodes, 1st February, 1453-4; De Lastic, Grand Master. Was again deprived for maladministration, 1459.
13. JAMES KEATING. Commander of Clontarf and Kilmainhambeg; nominated Prior of Ireland, *vice* Talbot, deprived, 21st October, 1459; and confirmed by bull of the Grand Master, Raymond Lacosta, dated Rhodes, 9th July, 1461. Was deprived of the Priory, for maladministration and disobedience, by bull of the Grand Master, D'Aubusson, dated Rhodes, 18th December, 1482.
14. MARMADUKE LUMLEY. Preceptor of Templecombe; nominated Prior of Ireland, *vice* Keating, deprived, by bull, dated Rhodes, 28th December, 1482; Peter d'Aubusson, Grand Master. *Ob.* A.D. 1494.
15. THOMAS DOCWRA. Preceptor of Dynemore, etc.; appointed Prior of Ireland by bull of the Grand Master, D'Aubusson, dated Rhodes, 24th October, 1494. Resigned the Priory, 1495, having been mutitioned Turcopolier.
16. ROBERT EURE. Preceptor of Slebeche; made Prior of Ireland A.D. 1496. Deprived of the Priory (suspended) for misgovernment and debts, by bull of the Grand Master, Emeri d'Amboise, Rhodes, 8th May, 1511. *Ob.* at Rhodes, 1513.
17. JOHN RAWSON. Appointed Lieutenant Prior, and Administrator of the Priory of Ireland, by bull of the Grand Master, dated 8th June, 1511. Confirmed Prior by another bull of the same, Rhodes, 15th March, 1513-4. Resigned the Priory of Ireland on being mutitioned Turcopolier, 27th June, 1527.
18. JOHN BABINGTON. Preceptor of Dalby and Rotheley, etc. Nominated Prior of Ireland by bull of the Grand Master, L'Isle Adam, dated Corneto, 27th June, 1527. Resigned the Priory on being named Turcopolier, exchanging dignities with John Rawson, reappointed Prior of Ireland, 1528.
19. JOHN RAWSON (again). Resumed the Priory of Ireland by request of the King, Henry VIII. Confirmed by bull of the same Grand Master, dated from "Our Priory House of the Hospital in England," 4th June, 1528; and re-confirmed by an

APPENDIX C 201

additional bull of the same, dated "Dover near the Sea, in England, *in domo qua in itineris Hospitali sumus*," 5th June, 1528. *Ob.* A.D. 1547.

20. OSWALD MASSINGBERD. Lieutenant Turcopolier; appointed Prior of Ireland on the death of Rawson, by bull of the Grand Master, John d'Omedes, Malta, 27th August, 1547; on condition that he, Massingberd, should not assume the title, or the Grand Cross, till legally in possession of his Priory. The Priory being confirmed to him by Queen Mary, he was allowed the dignity by bull of the Grand Master, Claude de la Sangle dated Malta, 2nd August, 1554. He afterwards resigned the Priory into the hands of Commissioners appointed by Elizabeth, 3rd June, 1558.

TITULAR PRIORS OF IRELAND

21. MATURIN DE L'ESCAT ROMEGAS. Named Prior of Ireland, A.D. 1573. *Ob.* at Rome, 1582.
22. DON PEDRO GONSALEZ DE MENDOZA. Confirmed Prior of Ireland by bull of the Grand Master, Loubens de Verdale, Malta, 27th July, 1582. Resigned the Priory of Ireland on being mutitioned to the Bailliage of Negropont, 1607.
23. DON DIEGO BROCHERO. Nominated Prior of Ireland by papal brief, A.D. 1609. Appointed Grand Chancellor A.D. 1613.
24. DON MICHAELE CALDERON. Appointed Prior of Ireland 1613. *Ob.* A.D. 1621.
25. DON PROSPER COLONNA. Nominated Prior of Ireland A.D. 1621. *Ob.* A.D. 1655.
26. ANGELO DELLA CIAJA. Created Prior of Ireland by papal brief, dated Rome, 25th February, 1666.
27. PIETRO OTTOBONI, Cardinal. Made Prior of Ireland by brief of the Pope, Alexander VIII., A.D. 1690.
28. ANTONIO MARIA BUONCOMPAGNI LUDOVISI. Created Prior of Ireland by brief registered in the Council, 24th November, 1741.
29. FRANCESCO CARVALHO PINTO. Commander of Portugal;

nominated Prior of Ireland by brief of Pope Pius VI. ; registered in Council, 20th June, 1792.

PRIORS OF SCOTLAND

There are very few records to be found regarding the Priors of Scotland, or Preceptors of Torphichen, as they are usually styled ; none are to be met with in the archives preserved in Malta before the year 1386. The names of the first four Preceptors are borrowed from various authorities.

1. ARCHIBALD. Named "Magister de Torphichen," in a charter of Alexander, Great Steward of Scotland, dated 1252.
2. ALEXANDER DE WELLES. Swore fealty to King Edward I. of England as "Prior Hospitalis Sancti Joannis Jerusalomitani in Scotia," A.D. 1291. His name also occurs in the Ragman Roll, as "Gardeyn de l'Hospital de Seint Jehan de Jerusalem en Ecoce." He was slain at the Battle of Falkirk, 22nd July, 1298.
3. RANULPH DE LYNDSAY. Is said to have succeeded the Prior Welles, and to have ruled the Order in Scotland till after the year 1315.
4. WILLIAM DE LA MORE. Supposed, from charters, to have lived in the reign of David II.
5. EDWARD DE BRENNE. Named Prior of Scotland and Receiver-General, in a bull of the Grand Master, de Heredia, dated Rhodes, 5th of June, 1386, granting a lease of the lands of Torphichen, vacant by death of David de Marr, to a certain Richard de Cornel.
6. JOHN DE BYNNYNGE. A bull of the Grand Master, Philibert de Naillac, dated Rhodes, 24th July, 1410, grants the Bailliage of Scotland for five years to John de Bynnynge, he being bound to pay certain responsions specified.
7. HENRY LIVINGSTON. Named Prior of Scotland and Preceptor of Torphichen, in a bull of the Grand Master, De Lastic, regarding the payment of arrears of responsions, dated Rhodes, 5th September, 1449. *Ob.* A.D. 1462.

(WILLIAM HULLES, ROBERT MALLORY.) A bull of the

APPENDIX C 203

Grand Master, Fluvian, dated Rhodes, 8th May, 1433, complains of the non-payment of responsions, mortuary dues, and other imposts, by the Prior of Scotland, and appoints Robert Mallory, Grand Prior of England, Administrator of the Priory of Scotland, to hold that office as his predecessor, William Hulles, Grand Prior of England, had held it before him.

8. WILLIAM MELDRUM. Is named Administrator of the Priory of Scotland in a bull of the Grand Master, De Lastic, dated Rhodes, 9th January, 1452-3, by which he is summoned to Rhodes to account for his maladministration. In another bull of the same, dated 24th November, 1454, he is called Preceptor of Torphichen.

(PATRICK SKOUGALL.) Administrator of the Priory. On the nomination of William Knolles he petitions the Grand Master and Council for the dignity of Prior, asserting that Knolles had been unjustly appointed in his place. The Council decide against him, but grant him an indemnity by bull, dated Rhodes, 3rd September, A.D. 1473. John Baptist Orsini, Grand Master.

9. WILLIAM KNOLLES. Nominated Prior of Scotland, *vice* Livingston [dead], by bull of the Grand Master, Orsini, dated Rhodes, 22nd December, 1466. Resigned the Priory, A.D. 1504; and died before the 24th June, A.D. 1510.

(PATRICK KNOLLES.) Named coadjutor of his uncle, William Knolles (in a bull cited below), who was incapacitated by age and infirmities from governing the Priory. *Ob. ante* 1500.

(ROBERT STUART D'AUBIGNY.) Nephew of the Lord Bernard d'Aubigny; appointed coadjutor of the Prior William Knolles, in place of Patrick Knolles, dead, by bull of the Grand Master, D'Aubusson, dated Rhodes, 17th March, 1501-2.

10. GEORGE DUNDAS. Appointed Prior of Scotland, on the resignation of William Knolles, by bull of the Grand Master, D'Amboise, dated Rhodes 1st July, 1504. *Ob.* A.D. 1532.

11. WALTER LYNDSAY. Received into the Order by the Turcopolier, William Weston, 31st December, 1525. Nominated Prior of Scotland by bull of the Grand Master, L'Isle Adam, dated Malta, 6th March, 1532-3.

12. JAMES SANDILANDS. Named Prior of Scotland in a bull of

the Grand Master, D'Omedes, dated Malta, 2nd April, 1547. Having adopted the Protestant Faith, he surrendered the possessions of the Priory to the Government, and receiving a grant of them to himself with the title of Lord Torphichen, founded the existing family bearing that name.

13. JAMES IRVINE. Is said to have succeeded Sandilands in the nominal dignity of the Prior of Scotland.

14. DAVID SETON. The last Prior of Scotland; retired to Germany with the greater portion of his Scottish brethren, about 1572-3. David Seton is said to have died about 1591, and to have been buried in the Church of the Scotch Benedictines at Ratisbonne. He was of the noble house of Wintoun.

APPENDIX D

QUALIFICATION OF SIR ROBERT PEAT

IN 1834, acting under the advice of the Vice-Chancellor of England, Sir Launcelot Shadwell (who himself shortly after joined the Order), Sir Robert Peat sought to qualify for office, and at the same time to revive the Charter of Philip and Mary before referred to, by taking the oath *de fideli administratione* in the Court of King's Bench. He accordingly attended on the 24th of February, 1834, and the Court, as the records of the *Langue* state:

"On its being announced by the Macer that the Lord Prior of St. John had come into Court to qualify, rose to receive him and he did then and there openly qualify himself before the Lord Chief Justice of England, Sir Thomas Denman, Knight, to hold exercise and discharge the office of Prior of the *Langue* of England under the Charter of King Philip and Queen Mary." The oath of Qualification taken by Sir Robert Peat in the Court of King's Bench is now a record of the Kingdom, and a copy of the same, authenticated by the signature of the Lord Chief Justice, is in the archives of the *Langue*. The following is the copy:

"In the King's Bench

"I the Right Reverend Sir Robert Peat Knight Vicar of New Brentford in the County of Middlesex and Prior of the Sixth Language of the Sovereign Order of St. John of Jerusalem in London do make oath and say that I will faithfully truly carefully and strictly perform fulfil keep and obey the ancient Statutes of the said Sovereign Order as far as they are applicable to the government of the Sixth Language and in accordance with the other seven Languages and that I will use the authority reposed in me and my best endeavours and exertions amongst the Brethren to keep the said Statutes inviolable this deponent hereby qualifying himself to govern the said Sixth Language as Prior thereof under the provision of the Statute of the 4th and 5th of Philip and Mary in the case made and provided.

"(Signed) ROBERT PEAT.

"Sworn at Guildhall, in the City of London, this 24th day of February, 1834, before me

"(Signed) T. DENMAN."

APPENDIX E

DIGEST OF THE CHARTER

The draft Charter received the Royal assent on the 14th day of May, 1888. The following brief synopsis may suffice. After reciting the humble Petition, the Charter constituted His Royal Highness the Duke of Connaught and Strathearn, K.G., His Royal Highness the Duke of Teck, G.C.B., His Grace the Duke of Manchester, K.P. (the existing Prior or Grand Prior of the Order), and certain other members who were Peers spiritual and temporal belonging to the Order, and the principal executive officers, by name, as well as the other members of the Order, of the grades specified in the Charter and returned by the Chapter as being on the Roll of the Order, and all persons who should, for the time being, in pursuance of the Charter, be members of the Order, one Body Politic and Corporate by the name and style of "The Grand Priory of the Order of the Hospital of St. John of Jerusalem in England" with a perpetual succession, common seal, etc. The Charter further declared that Her Majesty the Queen should be the Sovereign Head and Patron of the Order, and that on the Eve of St. John next following the existing Prior or Grand Prior of the Order should cease to hold office, and that on the same Eve of St. John His Royal Highness the Prince of Wales should become the Grand Prior.

In addition to Members there should be Honorary Associates and Donats—the Honorary Associates being regularly enrolled as such, and being under the government and control of the Order, as well as having a special Badge assigned to them; and the Donats being persons who, from an appreciation of the works of the Order, had contributed to its funds: of whom a proper list should be preserved, though they are not enrolled, nor entitled to any Badge.

All Members and Honorary Associates should profess the Christian Faith.

The Statutes as amended by the Committee appointed by the Chapter, including the objects and purposes of the Order, were generally confirmed, and Bye-laws for the further administration of the affairs of the Grand Priory were drawn up. Full powers were given to the Committees of the several departments of the Order to carry on as heretofore the various branches of the work, such as the Ambulance Department, including that great work of the Order of St. John, the St. John Ambulance Association, the Almoner's Department, and that of the Ophthalmic Hospital at Jerusalem, and to further extend the hospitaller and other charitable works of the Order.

As the Insignia of the Order were expressly recognized in the Charter, and were to be worn by the Members and Honorary Associates of the Order, it may be as well to point out that an alteration was made in them by the restoration of the lions and unicorns in the principal angles of the cross, and by the omission of the crown in the badges of Knights and Ladies of Justice, except in the case of His Royal Highness the Grand Prior and Her Royal Highness the Princess of Wales.

APPENDIX F

PART A

RECIPIENTS of the Medal of the Order before incorporation by Royal Charter.

The Medal of the Order, originally instituted in 1874, is by the Charter allowed to be awarded, as heretofore, for gallantry in saving life on land. It is circular, either of silver or bronze; on the obverse is the Maltese Cross, with the aforesaid embellishments, surrounded by the inscription "*For service in the cause of humanity,*" and on the reverse a sprig of the plant St. John's Wort, with which is entwined a scroll bearing the names "*Jerusalem,*" "*England,*" the whole surrounded by the inscription "*Awarded by the Grand Priory of the Order of the Hospital of St. John of Jerusalem in England.*" It is worn suspended from a black watered silk ribbon. The Medal can only be awarded to those who, in a conspicuous act of gallantry, have endangered their own lives.

1875. ELIJAH HALLAM, Miner, *Silver*; FREDERICK VICKERS, Miner, *Silver*.

1876. JOHN SMITH YOUNG, Deputy-Commissary of Ambulance, *Silver*.
CONSTANT VAN HOYDONCK, Mariner, *Silver*; HENRI TROUSSELOT, Mariner, *Bronze*.

1877. GEORGE GATES, *Bronze*.

1878. THOMAS ERRINGTON WALES, Her Majesty's Inspector of Mines for South Wales, *Silver*; JOHN WILLIAM HOWELL, *Silver*; ISAAC PRIDE, *Silver*; WILLIAM BEITH, *Silver*; DANIEL THOMAS, *Silver*.
GEORGE PATMORE, Hertford, *Bronze*.

210 HOSPITALLERS OF ST. JOHN

1878. STEPHEN LITTLE, Constable, Metropolitan Police, *Bronze*.
1879. ARTHUR H. STOKES, Assistant Inspector of Mines, Eyam, *Silver*; CHARLES MALTBY, *Bronze*; JOHN HANCOCK, *Bronze*; THOMAS DAVIS, *Bronze*; JOHN DAVIS, *Bronze*.
1880. HENRY SPAVIN, Stratford, *Bronze*.
GEORGE FREDERICK HARRIS, Captain 3rd Foot, "The Buffs," *Silver*.
1881. EDWARD MOUNTJOY PRICE, Ilfracombe, *Bronze*.
JAMES MCGOWAN, Inspector of Roads for the Borough of Birkenhead, *Bronze*.
GEORGE CLARKE, Corporal 95th Regiment, *Silver*.
WILLIAM MAGUIRE, Constable, H Division, Metropolitan Police, *Bronze*.
GEORGE EVERETT, Labourer, Gloucester, *Silver*.
1882. MARION SMITH, Widow of the late bandmaster, 94th Regiment, Newcastle-on-Tyne, *Silver*.
1883. THOMAS MCGUIRE, Labourer, Birmingham, *Bronze*.
ANNIE LOFTUS, Machine Operative, Stockport, *Silver*.
1884. ROBERT NELSON, Police Constable, Liverpool, *Bronze*.
WILLIAM CORSON, Police Constable, Liverpool, *Bronze*.
ARNOLD LUPTON, Leeds, Mining Engineer, *Silver*.
TOM ROWLEY, Working Collier, Barnsley, *Silver*.
JULIA HATCHER, of Marnhull, Dorset, *Bronze*.
1885. JOSEPH DOUBLE, Inspector, King's Cross Station, Metropolitan Railway, London, *Silver*.
ALBERT ABRAHAM (aged 15), of Condurrow, Camborne, *Bronze*.
ALFRED JAMES COXON, Plumber, Uttoxeter, *Certificate of Honour*.
1886. EDWARD CHARLES THOMPSON, Esq., M.B., M.R.C.S., Omagh, Co. Tyrone, Ireland, *Silver*.
WILLIAM HARDWICK, Police Constable, Kidderminster, *Silver*.
JOSEPH JOHN THORNBOROUGH, Railway Porter, Kidderminster, *Silver*.
JOHN PEAREY, Railway Porter, Chester-le-Street, Co. Durham, *Silver*.

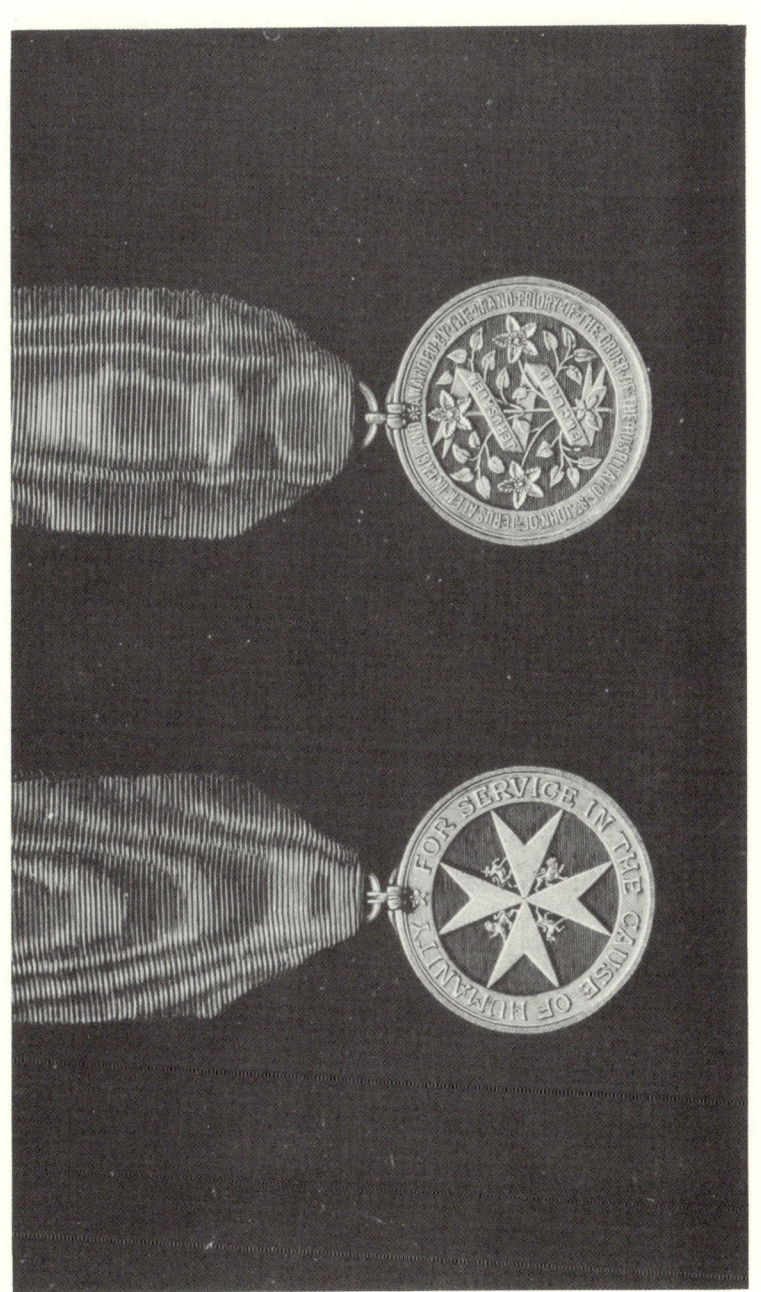

MEDAL AWARDED BY THE ORDER FOR SAVING LIFE ON LAND.
(After the Incorporation.)

APPENDIX F

1886. WILLIAM THOMAS, Mining Engineer; TALIESIN EDWARD RICHARD, Miner; LLEWELLYN PRITCHARD, Miner; GRIFFITH THOMAS, Miner; DANIEL THOMAS (No. 1), Miner; RICHARD JONES, Miner; WILLIAM CLEE, Miner; DAVID EDWARDS, Miner; DANIEL THOMAS (No. 2), Miner, of Mardy Colliery: *Silver Medal awarded to each.*

1887. HENRY BARTHOLOMEW, Police Constable, Metropolitan Police, *Silver.*

JAMES MILLARD and HECTOR THOMPSON, Workmen employed at the Elswick Steel Works, *Silver.*

PATRICK RYAN, Acting Sergeant, Irish Constabulary Mullingar, Co. Westmeath, *Bronze.*

1888. JOSHUA STONE, Police Constable, Hastings, *Certificate of Honour.*

PART B

The following are the recipients of medals and certificates conferred by the Chapter-General for gallantry in saving life, or attempting to save life, on land, since the incorporation of the Order by Royal Charter.

With a few exceptions the rewards were presented by H.R.H. the Grand Prior, at Marlborough House, until his accession to the throne.

On the 17th July, 1901, His Majesty the King, the Sovereign Head and Patron (acting on behalf of H.R.H. the Duke of Cornwall and York, Grand Prior, who was absent in the Colonies), presented the awards, and on the 14th July, 1902, H.R.H. the Prince of Wales graciously performed the same duty at St. James's Palace.

1890. THOMAS CHAPMAN, Pitman at the Drakewall's Mine, Calstock, Tavistock, *Silver.*

JOHN SMITH, Pitman at Messrs. Thomas Firth and Sons Norfolk Works, Sheffield, *Silver.*

Mrs. MARGARET IRVING, Holywell, *Silver.*

212 HOSPITALLERS OF ST. JOHN

1891. WILLIAM FEAST, Commissioned Boatman, *Silver*; and ALBERT KING, Boatman, *Bronze*.

JOSEPH JONES, 19 CR, Police Constable of the Metropolitan Police, *Bronze*.

RICHARD SMITH, Boiler Maker at the City of Birmingham Gas Works, Saltley, *Silver*.

E. SMALLER, Station Master at Bangalore, India, *Silver*.

1892. JULIA DIGNAM, St. Douloughs, Dublin, *Silver*.

BENJAMIN PARKINSON, Mine Burner, Clay Lane Iron Works, South Bank, Yorkshire, *Silver*.

THOMAS TURNER, Police Constable, Staffordshire Constabulary, *Silver*.

ALFRED WHITE, Police Constable 254 P, Metropolitan Police, *Bronze*.

THOMAS KIY, Railway Porter, Bekesbourne Station, near Canterbury, *Bronze*.

Major JOHN BARNET BARKER (late 75th Regiment), Chief Constable of Birkenhead, *Bronze*.

ROBERT ARMSTRONG, Police Constable, Liverpool Police Force, *Bronze*.

FRANK THOMAS LANE, Police Constable 554 A, Metropolitan Police, *Bronze*.

DANIEL RYDER, Crossing Sweeper, Westminster, *Bronze*.

THOMAS HENRY ROTHWELL, Police Constable, Liverpool Police Force, *Certificate of Honour*.

1893. Mr. JOHN WILLIAM HUTCHINSON, Manager, and Mr. JOHN FOSTER, Deputy-Manager of the Bamfurlong Collieries, near Wigan, *Silver Medal in each case.*

SAMUEL TABER, Labourer, Greenwich, *Silver*.

Captain URIAH COOKE, 2nd Cinque Ports Artillery Volunteers, *Bronze*.

ROBERT STOOPS, Railway Porter, Portsdown Station, Ireland, *Certificate of Honour*.

LEWIS LAMBERT, Coachman in service at Clapham, *Certificate of Honour*.

JOE ADAMS, of Shepherd's Bush, London, a lad aged nine, *Certificate of Honour*.

APPENDIX F 213

1893. AARON BERRY, Police Constable, 260 E, Liverpool Police Force, *Certificate of Honour.*
1894. ROBERT LONG, Wiltshire Yeomanry, *Bronze.*
JOSEPH DAVIES, Police Constable F 225, Metropolitan Police, *Bronze.*
WILLIAM MORGAN and ERNEST MADDOCK, Railway Porters, Metropolitan Railway, *Bronze Medal in each case.*
WILLIAM WESTLEY, Guard, North London Railway, *Certificate of Honour.*
1895. JOHN WATTS, Manager, Audley Colliery, and WILLIAM DODD, Under Manager, Audley Colliery, *Silver Medal in each case.*
WILLIAM MUGFORD and WILLIAM RAYMOND, Employés of the Corporation of Torquay, *Bronze Medal in each case.*
JOHN BOLTON, Miner, Audley Colliery, *Bronze.*
JOHN WILLIAM ROBINSON and SAMUEL WILKINSON, Railway Porters, Stockton-on-Tees, *Certificate of Honour in each case.*
JAMES JOHNSON, Engine Driver, Messrs. G. H. Nicholson and Son's Tan Works, Ipswich, *Certificate of Honour.*
GEORGE FROST, Wagoner, Audley Colliery, *Certificate of Honour.*
1896. JAMES HENRY HAMER, Duxbury Park Colliery, near Chorley, Lancashire, *Silver.*
THOMAS BROWN, Duxbury Park Colliery, near Chorley, Lancashire, *Silver.*
BENJAMIN HOLLAND, Gotham, Derby, *Silver.*
THOMAS WILLIAM CLOVER, Margate, *Bronze.*
CHRISTOPHER MURPHY, Police Constable, Glasgow Police, *Bronze.*
GEORGE JOSIAH HAYLOCK, Police Constable, City Police, *Bronze.*
FELIX CALLAGHAN, Glasgow, *Certificate of Honour.*
WILLIAM STEPHENSON, Station Master, Carlton Station, N.E. Railway, *Certificate of Honour.*

HOSPITALLERS OF ST. JOHN

1896. ELLIS ROBERTS, Oakeley Slate Quarries, North Wales, *Silver*.

CHRISTOPHER DENISON, Porter in the employ of the Dublin, Wicklow and Wexford Railway, at Dundrum, Co. Dublin, *Bronze*.

1897. JAMES RICHARD WILLIAM MAYNARD, Railway Inspector at Yeovil Junction, *Silver*.

ALFRED ROBERT LUCAS, Police Constable, City Police, *Bronze*.

JOHN JAMES THOMPSON, Police Constable, Halifax Borough Police Force, *Bronze*.

RICHARD GOLDBY, Police Constable, Staffordshire Constabulary, *Bronze*.

ARTHUR EDWARD DAY, Porter in the employ of the Metropolitan Railway, *Certificate of Honour*.

JOSEPH CONWAY, Police Constable, Metropolitan Police, *Certificate of Honour*.

GRIFFITH J. WILLIAMS, Her Majesty's Government Inspector of Mines, and JOHN KEWLEY, Manager of the Snaefell Mines, *Silver Medal in each case*.

1898. WILLIAM BENNETT, Police Constable, of the Birmingham Police, *Silver*.

HENRY ROWE, Warrington, *Bronze*.

THOMAS WHINCUP, Superintendent, West Riding Constabulary, Pontefract, *Bronze*.

ARTHUR JAMES SCOTCHER, Police Constable, Reading Borough Police, *Bronze*.

SIDNEY VOCKINGS, Porter in the employ of the Great Western Railway, at Westbourne Park Station, *Bronze*.

THOMAS WILLIAM LEWIS, Porter in the employ of the London, Chatham and Dover Railway, Shortlands Station, *Bronze*.

1899. ROBERT BAMBER, Stockbroker's Clerk, Streatham Hill, *Silver*.

Bombardier WILLIAM PHILIP HALL, R.A., Dover, *Silver*.

BENJAMIN TURNER, Surveyor's Clerk, Hayling, *Bronze*.

FRANK RUSSELL, Carman, South Hayling, *Bronze*.

APPENDIX F 215

1899. Private FREDERICK LEGGETT, 3rd Batt. Suffolk Regt., *Bronze.*
WRIGHT WOOD, Mason, Halifax, *Bronze.*
CLEMENT H. BRASIER, Railway Porter, Canning Town Station, G.E.R., *Bronze.*
ERNEST PIERCE, Railway Guard, Woolwich Dockyard Station, S.E.R., *Bronze.*
EDWARD EVANS, Railway Signalman, Portmadoc, Cambrian Railways, *Bronze.*
Police Constable JOHN REAY PRINCE, Liverpool Police Force, *Bronze.*
BASIL BUSHELL, Station Master, Adisham Station, S.E.R., *Bronze.*
CHARLES CURTIS, Ganger, Box Station, G.W.R., *Bronze.*
DAVID BINGHAM, Clerk at Headquarters, Central Police Station, Cardiff, *Certificate of Honour.*

1900. Miss STONE MILESTONE, Medical Practitioner, London, *Silver.*
THOMAS PRINCE MILLWARD, Police Constable, Liverpool, *Silver.*
SAM DAKIN, Inspector, Lancashire and Yorkshire Railway, Halifax Station, *Silver.*
HENRY POND THOMAS, late Gunner, R.H.A., now Ticket Collector, Metropolitan Railway, *Bronze.*
THOMAS CLARK, Porter, Furness Railway, Kirby Station, *Bronze.*
HERBERT LIVICK, late Sergeant, Military Police, now Caretaker, Aldershot, *Certificate of Honour.*
Corporal MICHAEL CHARLES HICKEY, Army Reservist, Royal Welsh Fusiliers, *Certificate of Honour.*

1901. Miss HELEN PRITTY, Cretingham, Suffolk, *Bronze.*
Corporal THOMAS MULCAHY, late 1st Batt. Royal Irish Regiment, 12, Barrack Street, Waterford, *Bronze.*
ADAM WATSON, Railway Constable, 30, Victoria Street, Lurgan, *Bronze.*
BENJAMIN FRANCIS, Sheffield, *Bronze.*
P.C. THOMAS HENRY HINES, Ipswich, *Bronze.*

1901. HARRY LUSH, Horse Driver, Southampton; JOHN GRIST, Ganger, Southampton; WILLIAM MOODY, Labourer, Southampton; ALBERT EDWARD JOHN ADAMS, Horse Driver, Southampton; THOMAS SMITH, Bricklayer, Southampton: *Certificate of Honour in each case.*

ROBERT COOK, Horsekeeper, 252, High Street, Plumstead, *Certificate of Honour.*

FREDERICK JOHN WATKINS, Printer, Walthamstow, *Certificate of Honour.*

1902. ROBERT LAW, JAMES DICK, JOHN SHEDDON, JOHN JONES, Miners, Donibristle Colliery, Fifeshire, *Silver.*

Police Sergeant GEORGE GILHAM, Kent Constabulary, *Bronze.*

JACOB DELMEGE, Land Steward, Rathkeale, Limerick, *Bronze.*

Police Constable FREDERICK WOOD, Metropolitan Police, *Bronze.*

HENRY TOOLE, Foreman Printer, London, *Bronze.*

Police Constable HEDLEY VICTOR SAYER, Hants Constabulary, *Bronze.*

ALFRED HUTSON, Jun., Superintendent, Volunteer Fire Brigade, Cork, *Bronze.*

Police Constable JOHN NICHOLSON, Durham County Constabulary, *Bronze.*

Police Constable EDWIN ARTHUR CHIDLEY, City of London Police, *Bronze.*

Police Constable JAMES NIVEN, City of London Police, *Bronze.*

ENOCH LUSTY, A.B., H.M.S. "Excellent," *Certificate of Honour.*

Police Constable PETER GAMMIE, Edinburgh Police, *Certificate of Honour.*

APPENDIX F

SERVICE MEDAL

The Service Medal was instituted in the year 1898, and was presented by H.R.H. the Prince of Wales, Grand Prior, at Marlborough House, on the 6th January and 11th July, 1900, and again by His Majesty the King, Sovereign Head and Patron (acting on behalf of the Grand Prior, H.R.H. the Duke of Cornwall and York, absent in the Colonies), at Marlborough House, on the 17th July, 1901.

1899. Sir JOHN FURLEY.
    Colonel SIR HERBERT C. PERROTT, Bart.
    Brigade Chief Superintendent W. J. CHURCH-BRASIER.
    Chief Superintendent JOHN HARRISON BUCKLEY.
    FRANK HENRY TURNER, Esq.
    District Chief Surgeon SAMUEL OSBORN, F.R.C.S.
    Superintendent EDWARD ROBERT GOODWIN.
    Assist. Commissioner FRANÇOIS DONALD MACKENZIE.
    Deputy Commissioner CHARLES JOSEPH TRIMBLE, L.R.C.P.
    Honorary Surgeon CHARLES HARRIS TAMPLIN, L.R.C.P.

1900. Deputy Commissioner STUART CRAWFORD WARDELL.
    Honorary Surgeon WILLIAM ACKRILL STAMFORD, M.R.C.S.
    WALTER ROWLEY, Esq.
    Major CHARLES R. FLETCHER LUTWIDGE.
    WAYNMAN DIXON, Esq.
    Chief Superintendent WILLIAM HENRY MORGAN.

1901. Chief Surgeon RICHARD BURDETT SELLERS, M.R.C.S.
    Chief Superintendent MARSHALL HOPPER.
    Lady Superintendent Mrs. PRISCILLA LAVERACK.
    First Nursing Officer Mrs. MARY JANE HARE.
    Private RICHARD SLATER.
    Deputy Commissioner CHARLES HENRY MILBURN, M.B.
    District Chief Surgeon GEORGE THOMSON, M.D.
    First Officer BENJAMIN SELLARS.

1902. WILLIAM HENRY IRVIN SELLERS, M.R.C.S.
    ARCHIBALD ALEXANDER GEORGE DICKEY, M.D.

218 HOSPITALLERS OF ST. JOHN

1902. JOHN PERRY.
JOHN GEORGE STEVENSON, Private, Northampton Corps, St. John Ambulance Brigade.
ALBERT EDWARD GORDON COX, Private, Northampton Corps, St. John Ambulance Brigade.
THOMAS DANIEL HIGGENS, Private, Northampton Corps, St. John Ambulance Brigade.
CLEMENT HEATHCOTE, Honorary Serving Brother of the Order, Superintendent, Winsford Division, St. John Ambulance Brigade.

INDEX

Aboukir, 96.
Acre, St. Jean de, 12, 14.
Agnes, Sister, 32.
Alban, Prior, 50.
Albany, H.R.H. Duke of, 141.
Albert of Erbach, Count, 88, 89.
Alexander, Emperor, 102.
Alexander IV., Pope, 7, 13.
Alexander VI., Pope, 26.
Alexandra, Queen, 141.
Algiers, 20, 75.
Almoner's Department, 145.
Amabilia, Sister, 32.
Amalfi, Merchants of, 2, 3.
Ambulance Association (St. John), 113-140.
Ambulance Committee (St. John), 113.
Ambulance Department, 109.
Ambulance work in India, 135.
Amherst of Hackney, Lord, 147, 154, 158.
Amiens, Peace of, 96.
Amicia, Sister, 32.
Ampthill, Lord, 137.
Anatolian Archers, 69.
Angleterre, Auberge de, 63, 84.
Anglo-Bavarian Langue, 64, 85.
Antioch, 8, 10.
Antonine Order, 93.

Aragon, Langue of, 18.
Archdall ("Monasticon"), 43.
Ardes, 37.
Army Nursing Reserve, 169.
Ascaneo, Corneo, 80.
Ashford litter, 123.
Athelstan, King, 3.
Auberges, 19.
Auvergne, Langue of, 18, 93.
Aylesbury, Earl of, 57.

Babington, Philip, 83.
Baillis of Aquila or Eagle, 194 et seq.
Baillis of Aquila (titular), 197-198.
Bajazet, 21, 26, 99.
Baldwin II., King, 6.
Ball, Sir Alexander, 96.
Ballyhawk, 37.
Baneby, H. de, 38.
Bangor, Bishop of (Alban), 50.
Banks, B. B., 177.
Barbarossa, Emperor, 69.
Barnes, W. G., 180.
Baroda, H.H. Gaikwar of, 137.
Bartlett, 94.
Basilia, Sister, 32.
Bataille, Commander de, 105.
Battenberg, H.R.H. Princess Henry of, 88, 142.

HOSPITALLERS OF ST. JOHN

Bavaria, Elector of, 100.
Beauvoir, Castle of, 10.
Benedictines, French, 3.
Belgrade, English Hospital at, 117.
Bertrand, Commander, 105.
Berwick, Duke of, 64, 84.
Beverley, Philip de, 38, 39, 40.
Blyth, G. W., Bishop in Jerusalem, 162.
Borgia, Count Alexander, 103.
Borgo, The (Malta), 76.
Bosio (historian), 61.
Botyll, Prior Robertus, 57.
Bourbons, 104.
Bowdler, Colonel C., 162, 179.
Bower, Sir Marmaduke, 62.
Bowman, William, F.R.S., 153.
Brandenburg, Bailiwick of, 103; Protestant knights of, 109.
Brigade, St. John Ambulance, 165 et seq.
Briset, Jordain, 30.
Buckland, 30, 62.
Budrum, Castle of, 21.
Bulgarian Relief Fund, 144.
Bulloin, Godfrey de, 3.
Burke, Sir Bernard, 103.
Burnet, Bishop, 58.
Burton, Lady, 152.
Busca, Count Antoine, 103.

Cabressa, 105.
Caesarea, Archbishop of, 6.
Caffarelli, General, 17, 95.
Candelissa, 75, 76.
Candida, Prince of, 103.
Cant, Dr., 158, 160.
Carac, 10.
Carretto, Grand Master, 27.

Cairo, Victoria Hospital, 142.
Casal Zabbar, 77.
Castel Blanco, 10.
Castile, Bastion of, 77; Langue of, 18.
Catania, 103.
Catherine II., Empress, 99.
Cavorsin, William de, 20, 25.
Cavagiali, Corsair, 76.
Caxton, William (printer), 25.
Centellès, Giovanni, 7, 103.
Central British Red Cross Committee, 133.
Chaplin, Dr. Thomas, 154.
Charlemagne, Emperor, 3.
Charlemont, Lord, 86.
Charles II., King, 66.
Charles V., Emperor, 29, 68.
Charles VIII., King, 26.
Chastelain, Chevalier de, 108.
Chateauneuf, Commander de Peyre de, 105.
Charles of Denmark, Prince, 177.
Chippenham, 47.
Christina, Sister, 32.
Christian, H.R.H. Princess, 179.
Christian, H.R.H. Prince, 177.
Christian, Princess, Hospital train, 168.
Church-Brasier, Mr., 180.
Citta Vecchia, 78; Cathedral at, 96.
Clanefelde, 32.
Clarence and Avondale, H.R.H. Duke of, 111, 142, 148.
Clement V., Pope, 17.
Clement VII., Pope, 29.
Clerkenwell, Prior of, 19, 40; Priory of, 30, 41.

INDEX

Clontarf, 36, 37.
Clontarf, Lord, 66.
Colloredo, Count, 103.
Commanderies of the Order of St. John in England, 182, 183.
Confraria, 35, 60.
Connaught, H.R.H. Duke of, 67, 142.
Conrad of Montserrat, 11.
Constantinople, 23.
Convention, Articles of, 106.
Conventual Bailiffs, 18.
Cook, Mr. John A., 160.
Cornwall, Duke of, 49.
Corradino, 75.
Corrodary, 38.
Cort, Robert, Preceptor, 39.
Cotgrave's Manual, 119.
Crook, 37.
Crusades, 2.
Cunliffe, Sir Philip, 149.
Curio, Caelius Secundus (historian), 65.
Currie, Mr. Donald, 108.
Curzon of Kedleston, Lord, 136.
Cyprus, Island of, 15, 16.

D'Amboise, Grand Master, 27.
Dame Chevalière, 101.
D'Amiral, 27.
D'Aubusson, Grand Master, 23, 27, 99.
Dauphigny, Nobles of, 93.
David, Tower of, 10.
David I., King, 36.
De Comps, Grand Master, 13.
De Gozon, Grand Master, 19.
De la Cassiere, Grand Master, 29.

De Milly, Grand Master, 23.
De Naillac, Grand Master, 21.
De Rohan, Grand Master, 85.
De Tybertis, Prior Leonard, 32.
Deutscher Samariter-Verein, 126.
De Vere, Gilbert, 32.
De Villanova, Grand Master, 32.
De Villaret, Fulco, Grand Master, 16.
Dingley, Sir Thomas, 61.
Dhanjethai Melita, Dr., 137.
Dienne, Commander de, 105.
Docwra, Prior Thomas, 50, 57.
Dragut (corsair), 69, 70, 71, 73, 74.
Dryden (traveller), 87.
Duckworth, Rev. H. T. F., 2.
Duncan, Colonel F., C.B., M.P., 110, 113, 131.
Duncan Memorial Station, 131.
Dynmore (preceptory), 47, 49.

Eagle, Bailiff of, 67; Bailiwick of, 38, 39, 40.
Eastern War Sick and Wounded Relief Fund, 116.
Eccles, E., 177.
Edward VI., King, 57, 62.
Edward VII., H.M. King, 171.
Edwards, W. R., 180.
Egyptian War, 142.
Ekkehard (historian), 3.
Elizabeth, Queen, 63, 66.
Elliston, Lt.-Colonel, 98, 180.
Elliot, Sir Henry, 149.
Emlyn, Lord, 131.
England, A., 177.
English Langue, 18.

222 HOSPITALLERS OF ST. JOHN

Esmarch, Professor von, 126, 127.
Esmarch bandage, 120.

Faxfleet, 49.
Ferrara, 103.
Fina, Prioress, 32.
Fitzgerald, Thomas, 65.
Foulkes, W. W., 177.
France, Langue of, 18, 91, 93.
Franco-German War, 112.
Frapant, George, 23.
Frederick, Emperor, 13.
Frederick William III., 103.
Freshfield, Dr. Edwin, F.S.A., 131.
Furley, Sir John, 109, 113, 116, 118, 121, 126, 132, 133, 134.

Gerard, 4, 6, 128.
German, Sir David, 62.
German Empress, H.I.M. the, 105.
Germany, Langue of, 18; Prior of, 103.
Gibraltar, Bishop of, 154.
Gille, Allan, 42, 43.
Gloucester, Dean of, 179.
Goleta, 20.
Gosford, 32.
Gozo, Island of, 69, 70, 71.
Gozon, De, Grand Master, 19.
Grand Priors of England, 185 et seq.
Greenham, 48.
Guyon, David, 83.

Hales, Sir Robert, 55.
Halicarnassus, Mausoleum of, 21.
Hamilton, Lady, 101.

Hamton, 32.
Hanley Castle, 110, 145.
Hassan of Algiers, 75, 76, 77, 81.
Henry VIII., King, 29, 50, 58, 59, 62.
Heraclius, Patriarch, 30.
Hexton, 3.
Hoggeshawe, 32.
Holbeche, Lt.-Colonel Richard, 134, 180.
Holy Places, 17; Governor of, 149.
Holy Sepulchre, 4, 5, 10.
Hompesch, F. von, Grand Master, 64, 94, 99, 101.
Hope, Sir W. Johnstone, 101.
Hospitallers in England, 109.
Houlton, Lady, 142.
Howard (traveller), 90, 92.
Hugo (historian), 30.
Hungary, King of, 14.
Hutton, Surg.-Major G., 145.
Hyrcanus, John, 2, 3.

Imperial Yeomanry Hospital, 168.
Infermeria, 89.
Isaac, Thomas, 43.
Islip, Walter, 43.
Italy, Langue of, 18.

James II., King, 84.
Janissaries, 69.
Jervis, Roger, 24.
Jerusalem, Bishop in, 158, 162; Hospice at, 110, 149.
"Jerusalem," Pierotti's, 6.
Jewel, Bishop, 64.
Johanna, Sister, 32.

INDEX 223

Kaye, John, 25.
Keating, James, 65.
Kemble, 32, 34, 40, 45, 46, 49, 109.
Kendal, John, 21.
Kennett Barrington, Sir Vincent, 109, 117, 135, 144.
Kerebrooke, 32.
Kew, A., 177.
Khedive of Egypt, 142.
Kiel, 126.
Kilbegs, 37.
Kildogan, 37.
Kilhead, 37.
Killara, 37.
Killbarry, 37.
Killergy, 37.
Kilmainham, 34, 36, 37; Prior of, 67; Priory, 65.
Kilmainhambeg, 37.
Kilmainhamwood, 37.
Kilsaran, 37.
Kinalkin, 37.
Knutsford, Viscount, 133, 136, 179.
Knutsford, Viscountess, 179.
Kuhn (American Consul), 101.

La Fere, Fortress of, 10.
Langeford, William de, 42.
Langman Hospital, 168.
Langues, 18.
L'Archer, Prior Thomas, 32, 39, 42, 45, 51.
Larking, Rev. L. B., 33.
Lascaris, 75.
Laseron, Dr., 117.
Laurence, Sir Richard, 101.

La Vallette, Grand Master, 70, 72, 74, 75, 77.
Layard, Sir Austin, 153.
Laymon, Surg.-Gen. T., C.B., 115.
Lechmere, Lady, 154.
Lechmere, Sir Edmund, 114, 139, 145, 149, 154, 160.
Le Roulx, J. Delaville, 3.
Le Sangle, Grand Master, 68, 70.
Leybourn, Nicholas de, 38, 39.
Limasol, 16.
Lincoln, Archdeacon of, 39.
L'Isle Adam, Grand Master, 27, 28, 29, 30, 58, 68.
London, Archdeacon of, 117.
Longeton, Hugh de, 39, 41.
Louis XVIII., King, 105.
Loyd, Lady Mary, 101.
Lumley, Marmaduke, 65.

Mahomet II., 23, 26.
Maignend, Prince, 36.
"Maine" hospital ship, 169.
Malketon, 32.
Malquinat, 5.
Malta, 14, 29, 32, 61, 63, 68, 69.
Manchester, Duke of, 111.
Mansion House Committee, 143.
Maple and Co., 171.
Margarit, General, 11.
Margat, 9, 12.
Marsa Muscetto, 74.
Marsa Scirocco, 70.
Mary, Queen, 57, 62, 63, 66.
Massingberd, Oswald, 66.
Matteo d'Aleccio, 80.
Medrano, Gonzales de, 71, 72.

Melleha Bay, 80.
Messina, Priory of, 28, 29.
Milburn, Major C. H. 180.
Military Equipment Company, 171.
Millisent, Sister, 32.
Mitchell, Simon, 57.
Modon, 29.
Monserrat, Marquis of, 11.
Montenegro, 116; Prince Nicholas of, 117.
Moore, Mr. Noel, 149.
Moore, Surgeon Sanford, 116.
Morea, 105.
Morgan, W. H., 180.
Morne, or Mora, 37.
Moseley, Mr., 168.
Mount Royal, 10.
Mount Schebarras, 71, 81.
Muristan, The, 6.
Musta, 80.
Mustapha, 70, 74, 77, 80.
Musurus Pasha, 150.
Mynchin Buckland, 31, 32.

Naples, King of, 102.
Napoleon Bonaparte, 94, 97, 99, 104.
National Aid Society, 110, 112, 117.
Negropont, Island of, 23.
Nelson, Lord, 96.
Neville, Ralph, 49.
Nincrioch, 37.
Ninnis, Inspector-General Belgrave, R.N., 180.
Northcote, Lord, 137.
Notabile, 69, 70, 71, 77, 80.
Nouri, Pasha, 118.

Ogilvie, Dr., 158, 160.
Oldham, F. H., 177.
Ormond, Duke of, 66.
Orsini, Grand Master, 23.
Outlawe, Prior Roger, 43.

Paciaudus (historian), 3.
Paleologos, 23.
Paris, Matthew, 12.
Parker, Archbishop, 65.
Paul, Emperor, 99, 101.
Peat, Rev. Sir Robert, D.D., 106, 108.
Pembroke, Countess of, 49.
Perrott, Sir Edward, 101, 109.
Perrott, Colonel Sir Herbert, 134, 179, 180.
Petronilla, Sister, 32.
Philermos, Our Lady of, 100.
Philip and Mary, 63, 79.
Philip the Fair, King, 17.
Piali, Admiral, 70.
Pierotti ("Jerusalem"), 6.
Pieta Creek, 74.
Pigot, General, 96.
Pius VII., Pope, 102, 104.
Pole, Cardinal, 57.
Popham, Sir Home, 101.
Porter, Major-General Whitworth, 1, 4, 37, 85, 91, 103.
Porter, Surg.-Major J. H., 116.
Portland Hospital, 168.
Porto Reale, 63.
"Princess of Wales" hospital ship, 148.
Priors of Ireland, 202 et seq.
Priors of Scotland, 202 et seq.
Protector of the Order, 101.
Provence, Langue of, 18, 93.

INDEX 225

Prussia, Prince Henry of, 127.
Prussian Order of St. John, the Royal, 104.
Puy, Raymond du, 5, 6.

Raouf Pasha, 150.
Rawson, Sir John, 66.
Recipients of Medal of the Order, 209.
Red Cross Movement, 112.
Renella Bay, 72.
Rhodes, 16, 19, 20, 22, 23, 26, 27, 34, 51.
Richard Cœur de Lion, 9.
Rogerson, W., 177.
Rohan, Grand Master de, 64, 91, 94, 98.
Rome, Bishop of, 60.
Royal Army Medical Corps, 167.

Saddlecomb, 49.
St. Angelo, Castle of, 68, 69, 71, 73, 74, 88.
St. Anthony's fire, 93.
St. Elmo, Castle of, 70, 71, 72, 78, 80.
St. Gregory, 3.
St. Jean d'Acre, 9.
St. John, hand of, 99, 101.
St. John Eleemon, Church of, 5.
St. John, Lord, 67.
St. Lazarus, 8.
St. Mary ad Latinos, Church of, 5.
St. Michael, Fort of, 74, 77; Tower of, 24.
St. Paul's Bay, 80.
St. Ubalesca, 14.
Saitteut, Bailli L. du, 105.
Saladin, Sultan, 5, 9, 10, 11.

Salisbury, Marquis of, 149.
Sandeo Alvarez, 80.
Sandys (traveller), 87.
Santa Maria Majora, Church of, 5.
Santa Torre, Chevalier C. de, 103.
Sapienza, 105.
Saplieta, 10.
Scrope, Chief Justice, 49.
Scutari, Hospital at, 118.
Senglea, 68, 69.
Selim, Sultan, 27.
Seton, David, 67.
Shaftesbury, Earl of, 154.
Sheffield, Sir Thomas, 21.
Shepherd, Surg.-Major, 121, 127.
"Shepherd's Handbook," 119.
Sicily, Count Roger of, 68.
Sieveking, Sir Edward, 140.
Simnel, Lambert, 65.
Slebach, 49.
Sliema, 72.
Smith, Sir Sydney, 101.
Smyrna, 20.
Solomon's Temple, 10.
Soltikoff, Count Nicholas, 101.
Solyman, Sultan, 69.
Solyman the Magnificent, Sultan, 27.
Somerset, Protector.
Southampton, 48.
Southey ("Commonplace Book"), 3.
Spahis, 69, 76.
Stafford House Committee, 117.
Starkey, Oliver, 63, 83.
Sterndon, 32.
Stowe, 57, 62.
Strangford, Viscountess, 117, 143, 144.

Straw, Jack, 55.
Stroud, 49.
Suardo, Bailiff Guévara, 102.
Sudbury, Simon of, Archbishop of Canterbury, 55.
Sutherland (historian), 100, 105.
Sutton at Hone, 48.
Sybbethorp, 38.
Swynderby, 38, 39, 41.

Tanner ("Notitia Monastica"), 31.
Tarschien, 77, 79.
Teaque Temple, 37.
Teck, H.R.H. Duchess of, 142.
Templars, 12, 17, 31, 32, 36.
Temple, Order of, 6.
Temple, Sir Richard, 154.
Temple Bruere, 49.
Temple Cowley, 49.
Templetown, General Viscount, 154.
Teutonic Knights, 8.
Thenegay, 32.
Thierry, Grand Master of the Templars, 9.
Tigne, Fort, 72, 73.
Timour the Tartar, 20, 21.
Toledo, Garcia del, 78, 79.
Tommasi, Count G. di, 102.
Torphichen Preceptory, 36, 67.
Trebigh, 47.
Tresham, Sir Thomas, 63.
Trimble, Lt.-Col. C. J., 180.
Tripoli, 10.
Tukes, Dr., 137.
Tully, 37.
Turcomans, 4.
Turcopolier, 18, 21, 64.

Turcopoliers of the English Language, 190 *et seq.*
Turkey, Sultan of, 22.
Tybertis, Leonard de, 42, 51, 52, 53, 54.

Valletta, 64, 82, 93.
Van Alen, Mr., 168.
Venice, Prior of, 51.
Verdala, Cardinal, Grand Master, 14.
Vere, Gilbert de, 50, 53.
Vernon, William, 180.
Verona, Congress of, 105.
Victoria, H.M. Queen, 109, 142.
Victoria Hospital, Cairo, 142, 144.
Vienna, Congress of, 97, 195.
Villeneuf, Elyan de, Grand Master, 51.
Villiers, John de, Grand Master, 15.
Viperan, John Anthony, 69, 75, 78.
Viterbo, 29.

Waddell, Dr., 154.
Wales, H.R.H. Prince of, 111, 147, 149, 151, 155.
Wardell, S. C., 180.
Wardino, English Hospital at, 117.
Warenne, Earl, 49.
West, Clement, 84.
Westminster, Duke of, 155.
Weston, John de, 39.
Weston, Sir William, Prior, 59, 61.
William III., King, 66.
Wilson, Miss, 160.
Winyard, H. G., 177.

INDEX

Wodehouse, 38.
Woodhouse, Rev. F. C., 1, 11.
Woolfe, Richard, 143.
Worcester, Bishop of (de Medicis), 29.
Wright, Ferdinand, 86.
Wysseby, 38.
Wytlefford, 39.

Yate, Major A. C., 136.
York, H.R.H. Duke of, 111.
Young, Colonel, 134.

Zacosta, Grand Master, 23.
Zanoguerra, 76.
Zebbug, 77.
Zizim, 28.

Soc
CR
4731
G7
B4
1978